through
the

LOOKING
glass

t h r o u g h

t h e

L O O K I N G

g l a s s

REFLECTIONS ON CHRIST THAT CHANGE US

K R I S   L U N D G A A R D

P&R

P U B L I S H I N G

P.O.BOX 817 • PHILLIPSBURG • NEW JERSEY 08865-0817

Unless otherwise indicated, all Scripture quotations are from the HOLY BIBLE, NEW INTERNATIONAL VERSION®. NIV®. Copyright © 1973, 1978, 1984 by International Bible Society. Used by permission of Zondervan Publishing House. All rights reserved. Italics indicate emphasis added.

Page Design by Tobias Design
Typesetting by Michelle Feaster

Printed in the United States of America

Library of Congress Cataloging-in-Publication Data

Lundgaard, Kris, 1958–
    Through the looking glass : reflections on Christ that change us / Kris Lundgaard.
        p.   cm.
    Includes bibliographical references.
    ISBN 0-87552-199-1 (pbk.)
    1. Jesus Christ—Person and offices. 2. Christian life. I. Title.

BT202. L86 2000
232—dc21

00-035617

To Karen,
my princess

Contents

List of Poems

About This Book

This book is about Christ. It's for reflecting on Christ through the looking glass of the Scriptures, relishing everything about him we can know, all his loveliness and wonder.

It's for anyone who is in awe of Christ and who loves nothing more than to revel in his greatness and wallow in his beauty. It's for lovers of Christ who are so taken with him that they want to lose themselves in thoughts of nothing but the Lamb of God.

It's for people like me who for a long time have had this feeling deep inside that Christ should be everything to them, their highest joy and crown—yet they've never been able to keep him in the center of their thoughts.

It's for people who want to be like Christ and try their hardest, but fail.

It's for newborn babes in Christ, just tasting the wonder of Christ, learning to take their first steps in adoring him.

It's for lukewarm believers who have lost their first love for Christ—people whose affection for him is a flickering flame that threatens to die.

It's for skeptics who wonder why all the fuss about Christ. This book is about Christ.

Christ with me, Christ before me, Christ behind me,
Christ in me, Christ beneath me, Christ above me,
Christ on my right, Christ on my left,
Christ when I lie down, Christ when I sit down,
Christ when I arise . . .

(from St. Patrick's Breastplate)

Author's Note

This book bears a striking resemblance to one by a seventeenth-century Puritan named John Owen. The similarities are purely intentional—his stuff was so good I borrowed it and bent it till it looked like my own. Still, his beats mine hands down. If you have the patience to learn to read his language (it's English, but not like we speak), I recommend that you put this book down and grab his *The Glory of Christ.* But if you haven't the leisure to learn a new language, I hope this book will do.

Owen isn't the only one who deserves my gratitude. I owe Maria denBoer and Thom Notaro thanks for their editorial nit-picking. Barbara Lerch's unquenchable good cheer makes the task pleasant.

I still have the notes from a class on the English Puritans taught by J. I. Packer at Reformed Theological Seminary in 1988. That's where he planted the seeds of my love for John Owen. And I offer Dr. Packer special thanks for his kind words and for smoothing over a few rough spots in this manuscript.

Paula, my bride, is my favorite reader of all.

And Christ, my Lord Jesus Christ, is the glory of it all— I thank you, precious Jesus.

For now we see through a glass, darkly.

(1 Corinthians 13:12 KJV)

We all, with open face beholding as in a glass the glory of the Lord, are changed into the same image from glory to glory.

(2 Corinthians 3:18 KJV)

Our faith, therefore, at present beholds God as absent. How so? Because it sees not his face, but rests satisfied with the image in the mirror; but when we shall have left the world, and gone to him, it will behold him as near and before its eyes.

(John Calvin on 1 Corinthians 13:12)

Lord, Thou art fulness, I am emptiness:
Yet hear my heart speak in its speechlessness
Extolling Thine unuttered loveliness.

(Christina Rossetti)

We start our journey by
discovering two unexpected truths:
There's a glorious Being who longs
for our company, and by seeing him
we will become like him.

To See His Glory

A lotta cats copy the Mona Lisa,
but people still line up to see the original.

—Louis Armstrong

THE COOL GUY

When he was still a freshman, Lex returned a kickoff
ninety yards for a touchdown against our high school football team. But our fortunes changed at the beginning of his
junior year when he transferred to our school. All the guys
knew before Lex arrived that he was fast. And all the girls
knew after Lex arrived that he was cute.

But Lex wasn't just fast and cute. He was warm and sincere and humble and respectful and kind and gracious—
and he was all this without being a square. Not only would
you want to be Lex's friend, but your parents would want

you to be his friend. He wasn't your ordinary teenager, nor was he your typical superstar.

In the first five games of the football season, Lex showed that he was destined to be all-state at halfback. But in the sixth game his season ended with the snap of his collarbone. That's how I got to know the cool guy.

While his bone was healing, Lex went to the gym every day after school to watch basketball practice. I was also in the gym every day, tossing around a lead-filled plastic ball on the upper deck.[1] When I finished I would go down to the court and sit on a bleacher near Lex to watch the team. Being a mere sophomore and about as socially gifted as a piece of decaying bark, I never said a word to this being who seemed to belong on Mount Olympus. Happily, he wasn't too cool to talk to me.

In the next several weeks Lex and I became friends. He invited me to his home, which I in my adolescence imagined to be a boon bestowed by this god only on his elect. Eventually I was honored with the highest recognition, when Lex invited me to come along to a Doobie Brothers concert in Albuquerque!

As this friendship ripened, I noticed that something was happening to me. My laugh changed. My smile started to draw up slightly to one side, rather (I thought) the way Lex's smile drew to one side. I started using words I heard him use. Even the way I sat changed—it was as if I was auditioning to be Lex's stunt-double. I was no Dana Carvey, but without the least conscious effort I was doing my best impression of Lex. You could say that I was being molded into his image.

DESIGNER IMITATIONS

When you admire someone—especially with affection—your heart is *warm,* or even *soft,* toward him or her. A warm and soft heart is like wax that is warm and soft—ready to take the imprint or image of something that is pressed into it, as a seal is pressed into wax. I'm sure you've noticed that when you find a friend who you think is the coolest thing on two legs, you start to adopt his or her expressions, accent, and hand gestures. You might even begin to walk or laugh the way your newfound friend does.

This happens because God designed us that way—to become like the people and things we love, whether good or evil. From our earliest days we are natural imitators, always being shaped by the things we hold dear—whether our parents, our friends, or rock stars. The psalmist is talking about much more than mere idols of wood and stone when he says in Psalm 115 that

> . . . their idols are silver and gold,
>   made by the hands of men.
> They have mouths, but cannot speak,
>   eyes, but they cannot see;
> they have ears, but cannot hear,
>   noses, but they cannot smell;
> they have hands, but cannot feel,
>   feet, but they cannot walk;
>   nor can they utter a sound with their throats.
> *Those who make them will be like them,*
>   and so will all who trust in them.
>   (Psalm 115:4–8)

Simply put: You become what you worship.

So it was only natural that I would start becoming more and more like Lex.

Ultimate Imitations

In the end, the Scriptures tell us, we who belong to Christ will be like him:

> Dear friends, now we are children of God, and what we will be has not yet been made known. But we know that when he appears, we shall be like him, for we shall see him as he is. (1 John 3:2)

We who have lived our lives here in frustration and weakness will one day become like the Lord Jesus himself. This is a miracle of God's loving grace: He made us in his image in the beginning, and we through sin disfigured that image until it was all but unrecognizable. But God, who is rich in mercy, will through Christ undo our undoing and recreate us in the image of his Son.

Think about it. We'll be with him. We'll be like him. Is there anyone cooler to be with? Is there anyone you'd rather be like? Is there anything better you could dream of?

But did you notice how it is that we'll become like Christ? Read the end of 1 John 3:2 again:

> . . . we shall be like him, *for we shall see him as he is.*

In that day God will remove the blinders of weakness and sin from our eyes so that we can see Christ in all his loveliness

and majesty.[2] Because we'll see him clearly, we'll love him
completely, for there's nothing unlovely in him. To the limit
of our recreated capacity,[3] we'll see the fullness of his nobility, excellence, holiness, righteousness, kindness, mercy,
goodness—every beauty that could make us cherish him.
And that fundamental principle in us, that we imitate what
we admire and become what we worship, will be fulfilled.
Adoring him with all our hearts, with nothing to hinder us,
we will be like him.

OUR DYING LORD'S LONGING

In just a few hours you will die in agony. What's worse,
you already know it, and you know that no governor in
heaven or on earth will stay your execution. Your friends are
gathered around you for a meal, which you know will be
your last together before you're torn from them. What's
more, you know that when the end comes, all of them will
turn tail and run as deserters.

That is what Christ faced, and, of course, none of us
could ever fill his shoes. But if I were in his shoes, I would
have been filled with self-pity. I couldn't have held back the
tide of resentment that would have swept over me as I
looked into the eyes of those who would soon betray, deny,
and desert me.

But listen to our Lord's words at the table:

> Do not let your hearts be troubled. Trust in God;
> trust also in me. In my Father's house are many
> rooms; if it were not so, I would have told you. I am
> going there to prepare a place for you. And if I go

and prepare a place for you, I will come back and take you to be with me that you also may be where I am. (John 14:1–3)

No chiding and resentment here, no self-pity or self-absorption—only concern for his friends and a decidedly tender longing to be with them. John 14:3 should make every believer fall on his or her face incredulous. This is the Lord of glory talking, the matchless King of the universe who could have anything his heart desires—and he's talking about going home to fix up some rooms in his palace so that his friends can come and stay with him. Jesus has shown love to his people in countless ways, but none seems more human than this expression of affection and delight. I weep to think of it.

Wanting to have his friends with him forever, Jesus turns to the Father and offers up his fragrant longings, as the high priest offered incense in the temple. In his love he makes this startling request of the Father:

> Father, I want those you have given me to be with me where I am, and to see my glory, the glory you have given me because you loved me before the creation of the world. (John 17:24)

Someone who didn't know anything about Jesus might read this verse and think him arrogant and awfully taken with himself. But those who know Jesus rejoice at his request. They know that to be with him and to see his glory is all that can satisfy them, all that can bring them peace. Without this no soul can truly rest forever. As a needle that has been rubbed against a magnet and placed on a floating cork will twist and bob until it finds north, the heart of the believer, having tasted the love of Christ, will not rest until it lands in the arms of Christ.

> You have made us for yourself, and our heart is restless till it finds its rest in you.[4]

When I found myself turning into little Lex, something more was going on than my affection for him—something else accelerated my transformation. The one I admired returned my affection. Because he spoke to me and took me into his home and invited me to the Doobies concert, I was drawn to him like a ten-penny nail to an electron magnet. When his affection for me met mine for him, nothing in me could resist the impulse to become like him.

In the same way, Christ's tenderness for us draws us to him in amazement and compels our hearts to be like him.

Two Ways of Seeing

Jesus asks the Father to let us see his glory. This request wells up from his love, because he knows that to see him is our greatest joy and gift—not just in the world to come, but now. It's the life and reward of our souls. When we see him, we see the Father (John 14:9). In the face of Christ we see "the light of the knowledge of the glory of God" (2 Corinthians 4:6). And as we reflect on him, we are transformed into his image:

> We all, with unveiled face beholding as in a mirror[5] the glory of the Lord, are being transformed into

the same image from glory to glory. (2 Corinthians 3:18 NASB)

The Scriptures distinguish two ways or degrees of seeing the glory of Christ. Paul makes this distinction when he says in 2 Corinthians 5:7, "We live by faith, not by sight." He is contrasting our lives "at home in the body" and "away from the Lord" (2 Corinthians 5:6) with our lives in the world to come. In both, our joy is to contemplate the beauty of Christ. In this world we see "but a poor reflection" of him, because we see him only by faith; but in the world to come we'll see him "face to face" (1 Corinthians 13:12).

When Jesus prays in John 17, his ultimate longing is for his people to be with him and to see his glory. Although he prays that their vision of his glory will be perfected in heaven, he doesn't ignore the sight of his glory that we can have by faith here and now. Seeing the wonder and majesty of Christ by faith here in this world should be our concern, because *only those who gaze on Christ by faith while in this world will ever see his glory by sight in the world to come.*

As I write these words, it is August, and the heart's desire of my 5-year-old son, Kristian, is to go to school. He wants to get on a bus and go to a big building with lots of other kids. He believes it would be wonderful. But he is only in love with something in his imagination; he has no real idea of what it means to go to school.

Many people are the same way with Christ. They claim to love him and long to be with him, but they couldn't tell you the first thing about Christ. They do know, of course, that to die and be with him would be better than going to the other place. But those who say they long for Christ, yet never gaze on his beauty by faith in this life, are only kidding themselves.

WHAT GLORY CAN THE EYES OF FAITH SEE?

When Jesus walked with his disciples on earth, they saw "his glory, the glory of the One and Only [Son], who came from the Father, full of grace and truth" (John 1:14). But what glory of his did they see, and how did they see it? It wasn't the splendor of an earthly kingdom, for Christ "made himself nothing, taking the very nature of a servant" (Philippians 2:7). They would more likely have mistaken him for a slave than for a mover and shaker in Palestinian politics. He had no place to lay his head[6]—much less a palace. And the disciples didn't see his glory reflected in a handsome face, despite all the movies and paintings we've ever seen. According to the Scriptures, the Savior didn't save anyone with his good looks.

> . . . there were many who were appalled at him—
>   his appearance was so disfigured beyond that of
>   any man
>   and his form marred beyond human likeness. . . .
> He had no beauty or majesty to attract us to him,
>   nothing in his appearance that we should desire
>   him.
> He was despised and rejected by men,
>   a man of sorrows, and familiar with suffering.
> Like one from whom men hide their faces

> he was despised, and we esteemed him not.
> (Isaiah 52:14; 53:2–3)

And the disciples couldn't have seen the eternal glory of his deity, because no one can see that in this world.

How, then, did they see his glory? They saw it as he was "full of grace and truth" (John 1:14). That is, they saw him as the Promised One who would come to bring the grace and truth of God to his people. And they only saw this by faith, because the only ones who saw this glory were those who "received him" and "believed in his name" (John 1:12). They saw the glory of the "Lamb of God, who takes away the sin of the world!" (John 1:29). This is the same glory we can see by faith today.

When we look on Christ by faith and see him as he is revealed in the Word, we can only love him more. Each view of him draws us deeper into the charm of love and delight. As John Owen puts it,

> Herein would I live; herein would I die; hereon would I dwell in my thoughts and affections, to the withering and consumption of all the painted beauties of this world, unto the crucifying all things here below, until they become unto me a dead and deformed thing, no way meet for affectionate embraces.[7]

THE TREASURES BEFORE US

Anything that Christ would pray for has to be good. When he prays for us to see his glory, we know there's something extraordinary in store for us. As we begin to reflect on that beauty by faith, we'll find the tip of the iceberg of treasures before us.

1. Gazing on Christ will give rest, satisfaction, and peace to our souls. Our minds tend to be full of countless perplexed thoughts—fears, cares, dangers, distresses, passions, and lusts throw us into disorder, darkness, and confusion. But when our best thoughts are fixed on Jesus,[8] our hearts will be kept holy, serene, and spiritual. For "to be spiritually minded is life and peace" (Romans 8:6 NKJV). Reflecting on Christ takes our minds off things below—things that aren't worth comparing to the great worth, beauty, and glory of what we see in Christ (compare Philippians 3:7–11). When we take our eyes off Christ, we become strangers to heavenly life, and live without the spiritual refreshment and satisfaction that God offers in his gospel.

2. Adoring Christ will whet our appetites for heaven. We know that in heaven we'll be filled with joy forever. But what will be the fountain of that joy? Nothing but seeing the glory of our Lord Jesus! The Scriptures repeatedly lay this before us as our promised treasure:

> . . . we will be with the Lord forever. Therefore encourage each other with these words. (1 Thessalonians 4:17–18)

> I desire to depart and be with Christ, which is better by far. . . . (Philippians 1:23)

To be with him is better by far because we'll see his glory (John 17:24), and by seeing him as he is, "we shall be like him" (1 John 3:2), which is the goal of our salvation and our joy forever.

Seeing God in heaven is called the *beatific vision* and is the eternal fountain of the life of souls in heaven. But we know that the essence of God—immense and infinite—is invisible to the eyes of our flesh. In fact, we'll never be able to see the essence of God, because we are and will always be finite creatures. So the sight that we'll have of God will always be "in the face of Christ" (2 Corinthians 4:6). In Christ alone we'll see the glory of God in his infinite perfection, and this vision will fill us with peace, rest, and joy.

We can admire these things here, but we can't comprehend them. When we talk about seeing the perfection of God in Christ, we're high in the Himalayas of thought, walking a knife-edge. We have to choose our words as carefully as we would our steps on that precipice, lest we stumble. Still, there is in believers a foresight and foretaste of this ultimate vision of God in Christ. We sometimes hold in our hearts, by the Word and Spirit, a sense of the unaltered glory of God shining out from Christ, which moves and saturates our souls with unspeakable joy. From this comes the "peace of God, which transcends all understanding" (Philippians 4:7). Christ, our "hope of glory" (Colossians 1:27), gives us a taste of the firstfruits of his heaven. Sometimes he even lets us bathe our souls in the fountain of his light and drink of the rivers of pleasure that are at his right hand (Psalm 16:11).[9]

Such heavenly pleasures are both rare and brief in this

life. But it's only our own laziness and darkness that keeps us from enjoying more visits of this grace. My hope is that through the following chapters Christ himself will seduce us with his beauty, and we'll surrender to him, feasting on him as often as we can.

3. Admiring Christ will make us like him.[10] If I couldn't help becoming like Lex when I was taken with his charm, how could I by faith take a real look at the wonder of Christ without being changed into his likeness (2 Corinthians 3:18)? If we have been touched by God's grace and truly know him, we can't escape the transforming power of a sight of our beloved Lord. Our view of him by faith is often weak and certainly never as clear as it will be in heaven.

The wonders of Christ lie before us. Even though we see but a poor reflection of him (1 Corinthians 13:12), what we can see and know of him will calm our souls, stir our hunger for him, and certainly make us like him. With so much to be gained, let's get on with it and start reflecting by faith on the glory of Christ, through the looking glass.

FOR REFLECTION AND DISCUSSION

1. Christ is the Bridegroom of the church, his beautiful bride. As his bride, answer the question posed of the beloved in Song of Songs 5:9: "How is your beloved better than others, most beautiful of women?" (In other words, what is it that you love about Christ? Be as specific as you can.)

2. Have you ever felt that you were bathed in Christ and in some sense given a foretaste of heaven as you gazed

on him by faith? If so, describe one or two things about Christ that you were taken with.

3. What are your expectations as you begin this journey? Make a list of at least three things you'd like God to do in, to, or for you. Now ask him to do them—for the glory of Christ.

That Where I Am, There Ye May Be Also

How know I that it looms lovely that land I have
    never seen,
With morning-glories and heartsease and unexam-
    pled green,
With neither heat nor cold in the balm-redolent air?
  Some of this, not all, I know; but this is so;
    Christ is there.

How know I that this blessedness befalls who dwell
    in Paradise,
The outwearied hearts refreshing, rekindling the
    worn-out eyes,
All souls singing, seeing, rejoicing everywhere?
  Nay, much more than this I know; for this is so;
    Christ is there.

O Lord Christ, Whom having not seen I love and
    desire to love,
O Lord Christ, Who lookest on me uncomely yet
    still Thy dove,
Take me to Thee in Paradise, Thine own made fair;
  For whatever else I know, this thing is so;
    Thou art there.

(Christina Rossetti)

*Chapters 2–10 are like a long
stretch of breathtaking vistas on
our journey. Each chapter is a
scenic overlook where we'll
stop and gaze at yet another
beautiful side of Christ.*

[2]

The Only Face of God

Was never face so pleased my mind. . . .
—Anonymous

THE TRUTH ABOUT EMETH

Could I be more arrogant and foolish than to begin a chapter by picking on C. S. Lewis? His writings have fed and enraptured my soul, but there's one passage in his *Chronicles of Narnia* that has never sat well with me. It's in the final book, the story of the end of Narnian history, when Emeth (whose name seems to be derived from the Hebrew word for *truth*) meets his Maker. His Maker is Aslan, the great Lion who is the Christ figure of the *Chronicles*.

> So I went over much grass and many flowers and among all kinds of wholesome and delectable trees

till lo! in a narrow place between two rocks there came to meet me a great Lion. The speed of him was like the ostrich, and his size was an elephant's; his hair was like pure gold and the brightness of his eyes, like gold that is liquid in the furnace. He was more terrible than the Flaming Mountain of Lagour, and in beauty he surpassed all that is in the world, even as the rose in bloom surpasses the dust of the desert. Then I fell at his feet and thought, Surely this is the hour of death, for the Lion (who is worthy of all honour) will know that I have served Tash all my days and not him. Nevertheless, it is better to see the Lion and die than to be Tisroc of the world and live and not to have seen him. But the Glorious One bent down his golden head and touched my forehead with his tongue and said, Son, thou art welcome. But I said, Alas, Lord, I am no son of Thine, but the servant of Tash. He answered, Child, all the service thou hast done to Tash, I account as service done to me. Then by reason of my great desire for wisdom and understanding, I overcame my fear and questioned the Glorious One and said, Lord, is it true then, as the Ape said, that thou and Tash are one? The Lion growled so that the earth shook (but his wrath was not against me) and said, It is false. Not because he and I are one, but because we are opposites, I take to me the services which thou hast done to him, for I and he are of such different kinds that no service which is vile can be done to me, and none which is not vile can be done to him. Therefore if any man swear by Tash and keep his oath for the oath's sake, it is by me that he has truly sworn, though he know it not, and it is I who reward him. And if any man do a cruelty in my name, then, though he says the name Aslan, it is Tash whom he serves and by Tash his deed is accepted. Dost thou understand, Child? I said, Lord, thou knowest how much I understand. But I said also (for the truth constrained me), Yet I have been seeking Tash all my days. Beloved, said the Glorious One, unless thy desire had been for me thou wouldst not have sought so long and so truly. For all find what they truly seek.[1]

Lewis is offering an answer to the sticky question of what happens to those who live and die having never known the name of Jesus. He suggests, if I read him right, that some might have served Christ unwittingly, even in the name of a false god, and because their service was really to Christ, they will be received into his eternal kingdom.

I'm not sharp enough as a theologian to carefully critique Lewis. I don't know what Scriptures or reasoning lie behind the story of Emeth, nor do I want to chase any heretical rabbits. Still, although I admit that the destiny of the souls who never heard the gospel is a tough question, I can't be happy with any answer that seems to make Christ himself and seeing his glory a matter of indifference. Jesus and his apostles go out of their way to make sure we know that Christ, and Christ alone, is the way to know God.

I tell you the truth, the man who does not enter the sheep pen by the gate, but climbs in by some other way, is a thief and a robber. . . . I am the gate; whoever enters through me will be saved. (John 10:1, 9)

No one comes to the Father except through me. (John 14:6)

Anyone who has seen me has seen the Father. (John 14:9)

For God, who said, "Let light shine out of darkness," made his light shine in our hearts to give us the light of the knowledge of the glory of God in the face of Christ. (2 Corinthians 4:6)

This is the first way we know the glory of Christ: that only he can show us God. In the face of Christ the church can see the nature of God, the divine person of the Father. Without Christ we know and see nothing of it. In Christ alone we know God's holy being (the terror and beauty of who he is) and his unfathomable mind (his unsearchable wisdom). Whatever fuzzy, imperfect notions we may have of God apart from Christ, we can't have the "light of the knowledge of the glory of God" that enlightens our minds and purifies our hearts. To know God we must see "Christ, who is the image of God" (2 Corinthians 4:4), because "the Son is the radiance of God's glory and the exact representation of his being" (Hebrews 1:3) and "the image of the invisible God" (Colossians 1:15).

It is Christ's glory that he is the great representative of God's nature and will to us; had he not come, God would have been forever invisible to us. "No one has ever seen God, but God the One and Only, who is at the Father's side, has made him known" (John 1: 18). Because he is God, the Son has always been the image of God the Father. He is in the Father, and the Father is in him, in the unity of one divine essence (John 14:10). When he became man, he became the face of God to the church (2 Corinthians 4:6)—he became the "visible God." This is the original glory of Christ, given him by his Father (John 17:1–7), and which by faith we may taste and see. And this is why Emeth's story unsettles me. If he can come to Aslan through Tash, could someone come to Christ through a mere idol? If we can just as easily know God through a false religion, Christ has no more glory than a golden calf.

How Was God Known Before Christ Came?

Before the incarnation God's people knew him by the revelation of his Word and the ceremonies of worship. This was the glory and privilege of Israel (Psalm 147:19–20). The church knew him, but they knew him as the God who lived in "thick darkness."[2] God represented himself in darkness to teach them about the glory that he would later uncover in Christ. Now, in the face of Christ, we see that "God is light; in him there is no darkness at all" (1 John 1:5).

Before the incarnation the knowledge of God was only twilight in the church. But when the Son of God appeared in the flesh, all the mysteries of God—his being, his existence in three distinct persons, all the glorious properties of his divine nature—were extravagantly displayed to everyone who believed. And the light of the knowledge of them obliterated every shadow in the church and blazed into the darkness that covered the world, so that no one continued ignorant of God except those who refused to see.[3]

The deepest longing of those closest to God has always been to see his glory. David longed and prayed to see God, although he could see him only in types and shadows:

> O God, you are my God,
>   earnestly I seek you;
> my soul thirsts for you,
>   my body longs for you,
> in a dry and weary land
>   where there is no water.
> I have seen you in the sanctuary
>   and beheld your power and your glory.
>   (Psalm 63:1–2)

God gave glimpses of his glory in Christ in the sanctuary, or in the ceremonies of worship,[4] and David devoured them like rare delicacies. How much more should we cherish the view of it that we may have with unveiled faces, although still as in a mirror (2 Corinthians 3:18).

But how? If we're left to ourselves, if we have no other hope but to try to raise our thoughts by their own bootstraps to the immensity of the divine nature, we'll end up like Agur:

> I am the most ignorant of men;
>   I do not have a man's understanding.

I have not learned wisdom,
nor have I knowledge of the Holy One.
Who has gone up to heaven and come down?
Who has gathered up the wind in the hollow of
his hands?
Who has wrapped up the waters in his cloak?
Who has established all the ends of the earth?
What is his name, and the name of his son?
Tell me if you know!
(Proverbs 30:2–4)

But in his kindness God appointed his Son to be his face to us. Let's turn to his face and begin reflecting on just two aspects of the beauty of God that we may see in Christ. In these we can see that Christ is the only face of God.

IN CHRIST'S FACE WE SEE THE WISDOM OF GOD

"Where can wisdom be found? Where does understanding dwell?" (Job 28:12). "Can you fathom the mysteries of God? Can you probe the limits of the Almighty?" (Job 11:7).

We can't see God's wisdom in its pure essence, but we can begin to sound its depths in his works. And his most excellent work is his devising the salvation of the church. That's why Paul celebrates his own calling to preach "the unsearchable riches of Christ, and to make plain to everyone the administration of this mystery, which for ages past was kept hidden in God, who created all things. His intent was that now, through the church, the manifold wisdom of God should be made known to the rulers and authorities in the heavenly realms" (Ephesians 3:8–10).

It seemed in the beginning that Satan had outwitted God (Genesis 3). By a clever deception he persuaded Adam and Eve, God's crowning creations, to rebel against God's loving rule. The result was death and decay that buried the world under its ugly weight, until all of creation groaned for deliverance (Romans 8:20–22). God could have overcome Satan by mere strength; he could have melted him with one blast of his holy breath. But how would that have vindicated God's wisdom? The question would have remained: Who is more clever? Satan, who craftily upended God's plan with deceit, or God, who resorted to mere force to squash his enemy?

When we trace the thread of God's plan as it is uncovered in Christ, we can't help but cheer as God makes a fool of his chief enemy. Satan and his cronies probably partied from the kiss of Judas until the stone over the tomb began to move. They were clueless, otherwise they never would have crucified the Lord of glory (1 Corinthians 2:8). We see God's wisdom in his patience and timing, sending Christ to the rescue at just the right time (Romans 5:6; Galatians 4:4–5). We marvel at how he resolved the problems of bringing filthy, fallen creatures back into his holy presence (1 Peter 3:18).

If we have any interest in God, any hope of the joy of gazing on his glory through all eternity, how can we help but hunger for a taste of the delicious wisdom of God in this life? All the treasures of this wisdom are hidden, laid up, and laid out in "Christ the wisdom of God" (1 Corinthians

1:24). And when we see the infinite wisdom of God in Christ, we see *Christ's* glory—the glory given him by his Father. For this is his glory, that in him alone we see the depth and breadth of the wisdom of God. It's true that all of creation plainly declares God's wisdom (see Psalm 19:1–6)—yet its voice is but a whisper compared to the thundering of God's wisdom in Jesus.

To see this wisdom clearly in Christ is *our* wisdom. Deep reflection on it fills our souls "with an inexpressible and glorious joy" (1 Peter 1:8).

In Christ's Face We See the Love of God

"God is love" (1 John 4:8). His eternal nature is love. But what do we see in the world? "The wrath of God is being revealed from heaven against all the godlessness and wickedness of men" (Romans 1:18). The world is filled with evidence of his anger and displeasure, so how can we know and see the glory of the God who is love? "This is how God showed his love among us: He sent his one and only Son into the world that we might live through him" (1 John 4:9).

Here we can feast the eyes of faith on the loveliness of Christ. The Father gave this glory to him: that with his blood he would write in large letters that *God is love*. For our sake alone, under no other compulsion than his affection for us, he took on our flesh. He gladly despised shame and humiliation that he didn't deserve. He bared his back for a whip, bowed his head for a miserable crown, and stretched out his hands to receive the nails. All this for us. All this in love. And all this so that "in everything he might have the supremacy"

(Colossians 1:18). Do you see how excellent, how beautiful, how glorious and desirable he is? In him we have the most joyful sight of God that any creature can see. Any notion of God's love that we glean from nature or the works of providence is precious; still, we can't know from them that *God is love*. In declaring that God is love, Christ is supreme.

THE TREASURE HIDDEN IN THE FIELD

In these brief scribblings we've only lifted a finger to point to the glory of Christ in his being God's face to us— and we've seen two grainy Polaroids of God's wisdom and love in him. But God promised through Isaiah, speaking of the days of the new covenant, that our "eyes will see the king in his beauty" (Isaiah 33:17)—we'll gaze on the glory of Christ in its luster and magnificence. To reflect on this beauty of the King of saints is the work of faith. And who can measure this privilege: that we who are born in darkness and who deserved to be cast out into utter darkness have been transported into this marvelous "light of the knowledge of the glory of God in the face of Christ"? What are all the stained glories, the fading beauties of this world? Pile them all in a bucket and weigh them in the balance against one glimpse of God's face in Christ—they will be as a feather to an elephant.

Wondrous as it is, how many of us give five minutes a day to the admiration of Christ?

Thoughts of this glory of Christ are too high or too deep for us. We won't stretch our faith to reach up to them or hunker down to dig into them. When some sweet image of

Christ as our tender husband begins to flit across the television screen of our minds, we quickly interrupt this program for an important announcement. Within a few minutes we somehow weary with glimpses of Christ—even though such visions are supposed to feed our souls through all eternity.

Isn't this simply because our thoughts and affections are tuned to a different channel? Our minds are accustomed to other entertainment and aren't in shape for the faith-work of reflecting on Christ. That may be why most of us live at low spiritual tide, powerless and joyless in our religion.

But if we were in love with Christ, so that we couldn't wait to see him again—and if we were in the spiritual habit of gazing on him and marveling at him—then our lives before God would be sweeter to us. Day by day our spirits would grow stronger. We would more faithfully represent Christ to the world. Strange as it sounds, death would begin to sound inviting to us, as the final release from everything that distracts us from the sight of our Lord.

We have to prize seeing the glory of God in the face of Christ as the greatest privilege in this life. It is the dawn of heaven and the firstfruits of eternal life—in fact, this is eternal life: that they may know the only true God, and Jesus Christ whom he sent (John 17:3). Unless you esteem it as such a privilege, you will not enjoy it; and anything you don't value according to its worth you despise. It's not enough to consider it a privilege and an advantage—you have to value it above *everything.* Your soul has to yearn and faint for it; your heart and your flesh have to cry out for a taste of the living God (Psalm 84:2), or you'll be forever a stranger to his glory.

C. S. Lewis was mistaken in trying to rescue those who

never hear the gospel. But he knew the glory of Christ—he knew that Christ was the bright morning Star, the only face of God to us:

> We must think of the Son always, so to speak, streaming from the Father, like light from a lamp, or heat from a fire, or thoughts from a mind. He is the self-expression of the Father—what the Father has to say. And there never was a time when He wasn't saying it.[5]

For Reflection and Discussion

1. Christ is the Bridegroom of the church, his beautiful bride. As his bride, answer the question posed of the beloved in Song of Songs 5:9: "How is your beloved better than others, most beautiful of women?" (Yes, you've seen this question before. You'll see it again. And again. Each time you see it, try to answer based on your reflections from that chapter.)

2. Read Exodus 33. What can you learn from Moses about getting a view of the glory of God?

3. One reason we don't more often gaze on the glory of God in the face of Christ is that we don't know how. John Owen suggests that we might have something to learn from our "vicious habits"—from the way we ruminate on worldly things that lead us away from God. Take some time to weigh how some unholy object carries your mind away (be careful here: try to be specific, without soiling your spirit). How do you feed that hunger in your imagination? Write down a few ideas. Is there anything here you can turn right side

up, and use to learn how to be carried away with the glory of Christ?

4. Make a list of at least five aspects of the way God worked out our salvation in Christ (such as appointing a mediator who was both God and man). How does each show his wisdom?

5. Read one or more of the following stories from the life of Christ: Matthew 9:1–8; Matthew 12:1–14; Matthew 12:22–37; Matthew 21:23–27. For each episode, describe how Christ showed his wisdom—and how his wisdom is supreme.

6. Using your answer to question 4 or 5, compose a prayer to Christ, praising him as the one who reveals the wisdom of God. You may want to fashion your prayer in the form of "narrative praise"—telling Christ a story of his own greatness modeled after Exodus 15:1–18.[6]

[3]

Lost in a Mystery

I love to lose myself in a mystery;
to pursue my reason to an O altitudo![1]
—Sir Thomas Browne

WHO IS THE GOD OF THE STORM?

Religions always have to answer a basic question: Who is
the god that brings the rain to water the earth and feed his
creatures? On Mount Carmel, when Elijah had his show-
down with the prophets of Baal, this was the disputed point
(1 Kings 18:16–46). God had held back the rain for years
and dried up the land because of the sins of the people; but
now he wanted to reveal his power. He had Elijah challenge
the prophets of Baal to a duel to see who could bring fire
from heaven (that is, the lightning of the storm). Four hundred fifty prophets of Baal prayed their hearts out, sacrificed

a bull, danced until they dropped, slashed themselves with swords and spears, and shouted themselves hoarse. They begged Baal, their candidate for god of the storm, to send a thunderbolt to burn their offering on the altar. But the only sound they heard was Elijah's taunting.

When Elijah prayed to his God, a fire-bolt fell from heaven and consumed the offering and the altar itself. Then "the sky grew black with clouds, the wind rose, a heavy rain came" (1 Kings 18:45).

Over and over in the Old Testament the God of Israel is declared and shown to be the God of the storm:

> The seas have lifted up, O LORD,
> the seas have lifted up their voice;
> the seas have lifted up their pounding waves.
> Mightier than the thunder of the great waters,
> mightier than the breakers of the sea—
> the LORD on high is mighty.
> (Psalm 93:3–4)

> Then they cried out to the LORD in their trouble,
> and he brought them out of their distress.
> He stilled the storm to a whisper;
> the waves of the sea were hushed.
> They were glad when it grew calm,
> and he guided them to their desired haven.
> (Psalm 107:28–30)[2]

There's no debate: The God of the Old Testament is the God of the storm.

THE KITTEN OR THE THUNDERSTORM?

Jesus' disciples had no idea what they were in for when they followed him into the boat (Matthew 8:23–27). When a storm swept down on the lake and the waves threatened to sink them, they looked death in the face and their knees knocked. Their shrieking woke Jesus, who was napping in the boat. Jesus stood up. Without praying to anyone, he spoke to the storm—and the wind wilted and the sea turned to glass.

Now the disciples were *really* scared. Who was this in the boat with them? These faithful Jewish believers knew the Scriptures and had no doubts about the identity of the God of the storm. A minute earlier they had seen this Jesus as someone much like them asleep in the boat. But now, Matthew tells us,

> The men were amazed and asked, "What kind of man is this? Even the winds and the waves obey him!" (Matthew 8:27)

There's a passage in C. S. Lewis's children's story *The Lion, The Witch, and The Wardrobe*[3] that captures some of the confusion these men must have felt. It's just after the resurrection, and Aslan (the lion who is the Christ figure) appears to the two girls, Lucy and Susan.

> "Oh, children," said the Lion, "I feel my strength coming back to me. Oh, children, catch me if you can!" He stood for a second, his eyes very bright, his limbs quivering, lashing himself with his tail. Then

he made a leap high over their heads and landed on the other side of the Table. Laughing, though she didn't know why, Lucy scrambled over to reach him. Aslan leaped again. A mad chase began. Round and round the hill-top he led them, now hopelessly out of their reach, now letting them almost catch his tail, now diving between them, now tossing them in the air with his huge and beautifully velveted paws and catching them again, and now stopping unexpectedly so that all three of them rolled over together in a happy laughing heap of fur and arms and legs. It was such a romp as no one has ever had except in Narnia; *and whether it was more like playing with a thunderstorm or playing with a kitten Lucy never could make up her mind.*[4]

The kitten or the thunderstorm? Is Jesus man, or is he God? Is he our friend, made of the same stuff as we are, walking beside us, struggling under the weakness of humanity as we are, or is he enthroned above the heavens, all-powerful, awesome, terrible, sovereign?

The Bible's answer is "Yes."

In Christ, in one person, there are two distinct natures. One is eternal, infinite, immense, almighty—the form and essence of God; the other begins in time, and is finite, limited, and confined to a certain place. This second nature is ours, which he took on when he "became flesh and lived for a while among us" (John 1:14). There's no one else like him—and in this mystery he is glorious. In fact, this glory of his blazes so brightly that the blind world can't bear the light and beauty of it. Most people openly deny the incarnation of the Son of God.

This is the glory that the angels bend down to get a glimpse of (1 Peter 1:12). This glory is laid as the foundation of the church (Matthew 16:16–19). Yet we can't explain this glory to our children. We run short of words and analogies. Here we have to fall down and worship the Author of this wonderful mystery and, submitting our understanding to the obedience of faith, humbly adore what we can't comprehend.

O ALTITUDO!

My purpose here isn't to detail the nuances of the mystery of Christ as the God-man. I trust you to explore it as part of your growth in your knowledge of him.[5] My business now is to stir up your mind to contemplate the glory of Christ as God and man in one person.

First, fix in your soul and mind that this holy secret of Christ as God and man is the best, the most noble, useful, beneficial subject you could think of.[6] What is everything else compared to knowing Christ? Paul deems it all "rubbish" (Philippians 3:8–10).

What do most people think about and cherish? According to the psalmist, "Many are asking, 'Who can show us any good?' " (Psalm 4:6). That is, most people want to know who will help them get the things of this world and give them peace of mind. But the psalmist says, "Let the light of your face shine upon us, O LORD. You have filled my heart with greater joy than when their grain and new wine abound"

(Psalm 4:6–7). Nothing in this world can compare with seeing the light of God's glory in the face of the eternal God-man.

Consider the desirable things of this life: wives and husbands, children, possessions, advancement, power, friends, and honor. Is there anyone who's indifferent to these? But anyone who has had the least glimpse of the glory of Christ the God-man will say,

> Whom have I in heaven but you?
> And earth has nothing I desire besides you.
> (Psalm 73:25)

Others aren't so consumed by the flesh, but reflect on the wonder of God's creation and providence, as we should. But even in creation and providence there's nothing to compare to the glory of the mysterious God-man. Think of God's masterful handiwork in the galaxies and atoms; let the wonder of how he shapes kingdoms to do his will carry you away. But don't stop there. Come farther up and farther in—lift your thoughts to Christ as God and man.

Second, diligently study the Scriptures to see how Christ's glory as the God-man is revealed. You can't see it by the mere creativity of your imagination; it's a vision of faith searching God's revelation. Consider the example of the saints of the Old Testament:

> . . . the prophets, who spoke of the grace that was to come to you, searched intently and with the greatest care, trying to find out the time and circumstances

to which the Spirit of Christ in them was pointing when he predicted the sufferings of Christ and the glories that would follow. It was revealed to them that they were not serving themselves but you, when they spoke of the things that have now been told you by those who have preached the gospel to you by the Holy Spirit sent from heaven. Even angels long to look into these things. (1 Peter 1:10–13)

Keep this principle in mind no matter which page of the Bible you're reading: The revelation and knowledge of Christ and his work is the foundation of everything said by the prophets and apostles to strengthen us (Ephesians 2:20–22). This is the way Jesus taught the Scriptures on the road to Emmaus:

"Did not the Christ have to suffer these things and then enter his glory?" And beginning with Moses and all the Prophets, he explained to them what was said in all the Scriptures concerning himself. . . . Then he opened their minds so they could understand the Scriptures. (Luke 24:25–26, 45)

There are enough revelations of the person and glory of Christ treasured up in the Scriptures from beginning to end to exercise your faith and your meditations until the end of time.

There are three ways that the glory of Christ is represented to us in the Scriptures. First, there are direct descriptions of his glorious person and incarnation.[7] Second, innumerable prophecies, promises, and explicit instructions concerning him lead us to reflect on his glory.[8] Third, the Scriptures show the glory of Christ by the sacred ceremonies of divine worship under the Old Testament, as we'll see later in chapter 8.

Consider one example from the Old Testament—Isaiah's vision:

> In the year that King Uzziah died, I saw the Lord seated on a throne, high and exalted, and the train of his robe filled the temple. Above him were seraphs, each with six wings: With two wings they covered their faces, with two they covered their feet, and with two they were flying. And they were calling to one another:
>
> "Holy, holy, holy is the LORD Almighty;
> the whole earth is full of his glory.
> (Isaiah 6:1–2)

Isaiah saw the glory of the divine presence of Christ filling his human nature, the temple of his body, with a train of all-glorious graces (compare John 12:41). And if this shadow of glory was so wondrous and holy that the seraphs covered their faces, how much more glorious is it in itself, as it is plainly displayed in the gospel!

Hunt for these visions of Christ's glory as you would for the pearl of great price (Matthew 13:45–46). The Scriptures are the field where the pearl has been hidden. Every truth in the Bible is for the good of our souls, a pearl to make us richer; but when we uncover this pricey pearl, the glory of Christ, we cling to it with joy. Then we find food for our souls in the Word of truth, and we taste how gracious the Lord is. The Scriptures are as refreshing to our hearts as a spring of living water is to our bodies.

Third, think often of Christ as the God-man. To fail here is a fundamental mistake that keeps many of us spiritually impotent, ignorant of our privileges in the gospel. We hear of the doctrines of Christ and say we believe them, but never solemnly meditate on them. The mind must be spiritual and holy, not entangled with the things of this world, in order to meditate on the glory of Christ. That's why most of us are strangers to this kind of meditation—we won't trouble ourselves to put to death our flesh (Romans 8:6).[9]

Some who seem to be sincere believers never stop to meditate on Christ and his glory. Oddly, they claim that they want nothing more than to see his glory in heaven forever. How can we reconcile this? It's impossible for someone who never delights to reflect on the glory of Christ as it is revealed in the Scriptures to truly long for it in heaven. How can someone find time to think about every silly thing under the sun, but never seem to have the time or inclination to raise a single thought to the Son?

Fourth, don't go long without thoughts of Christ as the God-man. Christ is near us—even within our hearts (Romans 10:6–8). Any time we turn to him, we'll find him ready to commune with us; that is, with the knowledge of Christ that we have from reading and meditating on the Word, we may have sudden, sweet thoughts of him through the day. And to let us know how near he is and how tenderly he longs to commune with us, he says,

> Here I am! I stand at the door and knock. If anyone hears my voice and opens the door, I will come in and eat with him, and he with me. (Revelation 3:20)

But sometimes, to test our faith or because of our sinful neglect, he withdraws from us so that we can't hear his voice, or see his face, or sense his love, although we diligently seek him. When that happens, all our thoughts about him are barren, empty of spiritual refreshment. And if we learn to be content with such lifeless thoughts of him, our spirits will dry up and wither.

When we first suspect that Christ is distant, we should do what the beloved did in the Song of Songs:

> All night long on my bed
> I looked for the one my heart loves;
> I looked for him but did not find him.
> I will get up now and go about the city,
>   through its streets and squares;
> I will search for the one my heart loves.
>   So I looked for him but did not find him.
> The watchmen found me
>   as they made their rounds in the city.
>   "Have you seen the one my heart loves?"
> Scarcely had I passed them

when I found the one my heart loves.
I held him and would not let him go.
(Song of Songs 3:1–4)[10]

Our glorious husband, the Lord Jesus, sometimes withdraws himself from our spiritual experience, so that we have no refreshing sense of his love, no fresh communications of his consoling grace. Those who never feel his absence likely have never enjoyed his presence. But those whom he has visited with his love, whom he has refreshed, relieved, and comforted—they know what it is to be left by him even for a moment. They are distressed when they look for him but can't find him.

If you find yourself in this lonesome spiritual state, turn back to the Song of Songs and learn from the beloved. Don't give up your hunt for Christ in prayer, meditation, and mourning; in reading and hearing the Word; in public and private worship; in diligent obedience—until you find him or he returns to you. And when you find him, *never let him go.*

Fifth, bathe every thought of Christ as the God-man with admiration, adoration, and gratitude. The knowledge of the God-man is an ocean whose depths we can't sound. When we're made new in Christ, our hearts, souls, minds, and strength are enabled by grace to cling to Christ. By faith our minds discern the nobility and beauty of Christ; by faith our affections long for Christ; by faith our wills embrace Christ. We learn to admire, adore, and thank Christ. In short, we discover what it is to obey the greatest commandment of all (Matthew 22:37–38).

This love which begins in the new birth should grow through our lives and ripen until it bears its luscious fruit in heaven, when we join our voices with the whole church of the redeemed:

And they sang a new song:

"You are worthy to take the scroll
and to open its seals,
because you were slain,
and with your blood you purchased men for God
from every tribe and language and people and
nation.
You have made them to be a kingdom and priests
to serve our God,
and they will reign on the earth."

Then I looked and heard the voice of many angels, numbering thousands upon thousands, and ten thousand times ten thousand. They encircled the throne and the living creatures and the elders. In a loud voice they sang:

"Worthy is the Lamb, who was slain,
to receive power and wealth and wisdom and
strength
and honor and glory and praise!"

Then I heard every creature in heaven and on earth and under the earth and on the sea, and all that is in them, singing:

"To him who sits on the throne and to the Lamb
be praise and honor and glory and power,
for ever and ever!"

The four living creatures said, "Amen," and the elders fell down and worshiped. (Revelation 5:9–14)

My whole purpose in this chapter is to convince you that the doctrine of Christ as God and man isn't just a creed to affirm. This mystery is the glory of our Lord Jesus and reason enough to attract us to sit beside Mary at his feet rather than to be distracted with Martha (Luke 10:38–41). One glimpse of his double nature is enough to fill our hearts and minds with wonder, until we overflow in admiration, adoration, and thanksgiving, until our souls rise to an *O altitudo!*

For Reflection and Discussion

1. Christ is the Bridegroom of the church, his beautiful bride. As his bride, answer the question posed of the beloved in Song of Songs 5:9: "How is your beloved better than others, most beautiful of women?"

2. Although you don't need a graduate degree in theology to meditate on Christ as God and man, you need to begin with some basic theology. If you don't feel confident that you can see that the Bible teaches that Christ has always been and always will be God, and that at a point in time he became a man—*and* that he continues to be both God and man forever—then before you go on, please pick one of the following and use it to help you learn these truths from Scripture:

The Heidelberg Catechism (with Scripture texts). Study part 2, "Man's Deliverance," questions 12–19—and make sure you look up all the Bible verses.

John R. W. Stott, *Basic Christianity* (London: Inter-Varsity, 1958). See "Part 1: The Person of Christ."

John Calvin, *Institutes of the Christian Religion.* See sections 2.12.1 through 2.14.4.

Louis Berkhof, *Systematic Theology* (Grand Rapids: Eerdmans, 1939), 315–20.

3. Identify at least three obstacles that keep you from thinking of Christ throughout the day. How does each of them crowd out thoughts of Christ? What are some things you could do to overcome these obstacles? Set aside a day of prayer (and perhaps fasting) to ask God to bring these barriers down and give you a day of delight in Christ.

4. What fills your mind throughout the day? (Work? Fantasies? Lyrics of songs on the radio?) Why does it fill your mind? (Necessity? Lust? Repetition?) Now, what could you learn from this that might help you to fill your mind with thoughts of Christ throughout the day?

[4]

He Stoops Down to Look on the Heavens

Give me the lowest place. . . .
—Christina Rossetti

UNDER THE CALLUS

If you've ever hoed a garden without work gloves you know that rubbing the same place on your palm over and over will make a callus. And when it gets hard, you can prick a callus with a needle and feel nothing. A callus doesn't have nerve endings, so it isn't sensitive.

If you've ever belonged to a church where they recite the Creed week after week, you know that your mind and heart can grow callused and insensitive to the truths of our faith.[1] I confess that at times during the Creed I've even looked around to see who has it memorized and who has to read it—my mind obviously unmoved by the words marching out of my mouth. Still, there's a phrase in the Nicene Creed that I can hardly get past without something catching in my throat, or my eyes growing moist. Speaking of Christ, we remind ourselves that

> For us and for our salvation
> *he came down* from heaven.

Maybe his love is too close to the surface of these doctrines for me to hurry over them. I can't shuffle past his motivation: *for us.* Isn't this what grabbed Paul when he said, "I live by faith in the Son of God, who loved *me* and gave himself for *me*" (Galatians 2:20)? This is too personal to be a doctrine of the church. Doctrines are supposed to be dry and crusty, not tender and savory![2] And I marvel at what he did for us: He *came down.*

ONE GIANT LEAP FOR MANKIND

Sin is a vast ocean that separates us from God. No one can swim across it. Angels with flaming swords guard the locked gate, and no one can get back into the Eden of God's presence.[3] This is the miserable way things would have stayed forever if God hadn't given a mediator to span the ocean, unlock the gate, shatter the sword, and bring us back to God.

> . . . there is one God and one mediator between God
> and men, the man Christ Jesus. . . . (1 Timothy 2:5)

Do you realize how important it is that God himself, as God alone, couldn't be the mediator between himself and us? Of all the tremendous, gracious work he did for our salvation, he couldn't in his mere divine essence be our mediator. And of course there was no creature fit to be mediator—no one in heaven or on earth could fill those shoes.[4]

With no mediator in sight, the Lord Christ, as the Son of God, said,

> Here I am—it is written about me in the scroll—
> I have come to do your will, O God.
> (Hebrews 10:7)

These are among the first and simplest truths of Christianity, and in these ABC's of the faith we find a striking show of Christ's glory. But we won't see that glory until we consider just how far down that step was for him. We have to know where he came from, as well as where he landed, in order to appreciate his giant leap for mankind.

Our Lover's Leap

I have three sons. One is 15, another 6, and the third is 5.[5] You can imagine that the oldest is a bit mature to play the games the little boys like to play. Occasionally, though, the 15-year-old will build a Lego™ Submarine or Helicopter for the boys—and they bounce off the walls with delight.

Sometimes he builds these toys under duress—I enforce a sibling camaraderie, and demand this "kindness" of the oldest. But at unpredictable times he'll give one of his cool tank models to them, or let them play with his X-Wing Fighter. It's these latter episodes that thrill me, because I see in him evidence of love and selflessness. I know how hard it

is for him to lay aside his own interests and serve them—he
has nothing obvious to gain from it.

Sweet as this brotherly condescension is, it can't compare to the giant leap down that our Savior took in order to
be our Mediator. He didn't become our Mediator by luck of
the draw; his Father didn't impose it on him; there was no
outward force to compel him against his will. He took the
job of his own free will (see Philippians 2:5–8).

When we stop to consider how Christ came down for us,
he is glorious in our eyes.

Just How Far Down Did Christ Come?

When the Scriptures speak of God's excellency in rela-
tion to his creation, they describe him as incomparably high
above us:

> Who is like the LORD our God,
>   the One who sits enthroned on high,
> who stoops down to look
>   on the heavens and the earth?
>   (Psalm 113:5–6)

Did you catch that? God has to humble himself not only to
see us, but to see the heavens! This means he's really high
above us. And he is this high above us in two ways.

*1. God is high above us in his being, in his very God-
ness.* No creature shares the divine essence with him. In
comparison to God, all nations are a drop in the bucket—if

weighed in the scales against him we're dust (Isaiah 40:15). Isaiah even goes so far as to describe the nations as "worthless and less than nothing" (Isaiah 40:17). In fact, when we try to compare the being of God, who is the fountain of all that exists, with any of his creatures, we're left without any meaningful illustrations or proportions. A molecule of water compared to the Pacific Ocean is still infinitely closer than the measure of our being to God's. Everything we can say is only understatement.

So it's extraordinary when God draws close to his creatures. We can't fathom how low he humbles himself to do it. And when he steps down and embraces not kings and queens, but the dregs of society, we fall speechless before his grace.

> For this is what the high and lofty One says—
>   he who lives forever, whose name is holy:
> "I live in a high and holy place,
>   but also with him who is contrite and lowly in
>   spirit,
> to revive the spirit of the lowly
>   and to revive the heart of the contrite."
>   (Isaiah 57:15)

2. God is high above us in his eternal happiness in himself. God doesn't need anyone or anything else in order to be happy. The Father, Son, and Holy Spirit have always been, and always will be, eternally satisfied. Within the Trinity there is perfect love. But no creature is self-sufficient. We all depend on something outside us—we all depend on God.

The human nature of Christ himself in heaven is not

self-sufficient; he lives in God, and God in him; the human nature of Christ is fully dependent on God, as we are, to receive all good things from him. God alone lacks nothing, needs nothing. No one can add anything to God:

> ... he is not served by human hands, as if he needed anything, because he himself gives all men life and breath and everything else. (Acts 17:25)

Can you see yet how this highlights the glory of the Son of God? Think about it: If he was so infinitely and unshakably happy and satisfied in his nature as God, what did he have to gain by taking on our frail human nature? Remember that as God he is so high above his creation in his being that it's an act of humbling himself to regard his creatures. How much more is it that he took on our nature in order to rescue us! It was an act without the least self-consideration— because there was nothing at all for him to gain. It was the ultimate act of selflessness.

Just How Did Christ Come Down?

We want to see as much of the glory of Christ as we can by faith. In order to see his glory in his coming down for us, it will help to understand how he came down. Misunderstandings about this have pestered the church since the days of the apostles, so let's start by eliminating some misconceptions.[6]

1. When the Son of God became man, he never stopped being God. The Scriptures clearly teach that Christ was God from all eternity. Before time began he was *with* God and he *was* God (John 1:1). When Paul talks about the Son coming down, he says that "he did not regard equality with God as something to be exploited" (Philippians 2:6 NRSV). That means that before he came down, he was equal with God—which is the same as being "in very nature God," as Paul describes him in that same verse. And this is exactly what the unbelieving Jews accused Christ of claiming, and what they couldn't bear (John 5:18).

Being equal with God, "in very nature God" (Philippians 2:6), Christ "made himself nothing, taking the very nature of a servant, being made in human likeness" (verse 7). This is the stepping down that is so glorious: not that he ceased to be God, but that while he was God he took on that nature of humanity. Although infinitely perfect as God, he took to himself this weakened nature that was light-years beneath him.[7]

2. When the Son of God became man, he didn't change his divine nature into human. Some claim that Christ turned his divine nature into human, as he turned the water into wine. But where is the glory in that? According to this, his divine nature was utterly destroyed by being changed into human nature.

3. When the Son of God became man, he didn't make some new nature that was a mixture of divine and human. Some suppose that Christ joined the two natures together in a mixture, like Nestle's Quick and milk, to make some third nature that was neither divine nor human. Had he done this, he would have taken something away from the glory of the perfection of the divine nature. Again, what glory is there in that? There isn't the least "shifting shadow" of change in the nature of God (James 1:17).

4. When the Son of God became man, he hid the glory of his divine nature behind his human nature. If Christ never ceased to be God, and he never changed the nature of God, then in what sense did he "come down" with respect to his deity? Paul says that he "humbled himself" and "made himself nothing" (Philippians 2:7–8); that is, he didn't exploit or take advantage of his being God.[8] He veiled the glory of his divine nature in ours so that there was no outward appearance of it. The glory of his deity was so concealed that the world didn't even think he was a good man, much less the God of the universe!

5. When the Son of God became man, it wasn't mere appearances. One of the first heresies that infected the church immediately after the days of the apostles was that everything Christ suffered and did as a man was in appearance only—just like the angels in the Old Testament who, in the shape of men, ate and drank. That is, there was only an *appearance* of Christ in the man Jesus at Jerusalem; the Christ, they claimed, never suffered in the man Jesus. But the ancient Christians replied to these heretics, You have found an imaginary Christ, and an imaginary salvation.

THE GLORY OF CHRIST'S COMING DOWN

When Christ became man, he took our entire nature— he didn't turn it into something merely spiritual. He took real flesh and real blood, a real human heart that could grieve and break. When he suffered, when he was tried, tempted, and forsaken, it was just as you or I would suffer.

If I had an angel's pen I could never adequately express the glory of this coming down. It is the most unspeakable work of the wisdom of the Father and of the love of the Son—the boldest evidence of God's care for us. What could equal it? What can I compare to it? It's the sunshine of our religion, and the life-giving soul of the gospel. It carries the mystery of the wisdom of God above our reason and understanding—past the minds of angels—until it becomes only the object of faith and admiration. It's a mystery fitting the greatness of God (Job 11:7–9; Romans 11:33–36).

He who was eternally God, who was as much a divine person as the Father and the Spirit, who has to humble himself just to look at the things in heaven and earth (Psalm 113:6), took the nature of man to be his own. From then on he was no less man than he was God. To multiply the wonder of this mystery, he humbled himself to the point that he became a man who was despised and rejected (Isaiah 53:3; John 1:11).

I'm trying to describe this as it's revealed in the Scriptures, and we believers try by faith to hold to this as revealed. But when we come close to a steady, direct view of it, our minds give up and our hearts melt—the only rest we can find is to admire and adore what we can't comprehend. We're at a loss and know that we will be as long as we're in this world.

But get this: in our loss, as we stumble into holy worship

of the Son of God coming down for us, God showers his grace and benefits on us!

Here we find our sanctuary, our certain refuge. What do the distressed look for in a sanctuary? A supply to meet their needs, deliverance from all their fears, and a defense against all danger. Sin-hunted souls that flee their own guilt and God's wrath, who can't shake the shackles of sin, find their supplier, deliverer, and protector in Christ coming down to be their sanctuary (Hebrews 6:18). Do you feel the heavy load of sin on your shoulders? Are you confounded by temptation? Are you bent low under the oppression of any spiritual adversary? One glimpse of the glory of Christ coming down *for you* can support and relieve you.

Any time we look for someone to help us, we need to know two things: Is he willing to help me? Is he able to help me? One without the other might be impressive or sweet, but won't bring relief. But we find both in Christ. What will he not do for us? He emptied and humbled himself, infinitely stepped down from the prerogative of his glory in his being and self-sufficiency. Won't he relieve us in all our distress? Won't he do for us everything we need? Won't he be a sanctuary for us? And we have no reason to doubt his power to help us, because by coming down to be a suffering man, he gave up nothing of his power as God, nothing of his wisdom or grace. He could still do all that he could do as God from eternity. So as we see his glory as the One who came down for us, we worship him—and we find our sanctuary. We're "filled with an inexpressible and glorious joy" (1 Peter 1:8).

The next time you find yourself in church yawning through the Creed, stop. Think about the words. Think about what it means that

> for us and for our salvation
> *he came down. . . .*

FOR REFLECTION AND DISCUSSION

1. Christ is the Bridegroom of the church, his beautiful bride. As his bride, answer the question posed of the beloved in Song of Songs 5:9: "How is your beloved better than others, most beautiful of women?"

2. Why is it important to know that Christ has always been God, and never stopped being God?

3. Why is it important to know that Christ became a man—a real man?

4. In this chapter we learned that there's a benefit to us that comes from reflecting on Christ coming down for us: We find in him our sanctuary. Can you think of any other benefits that might grow out of such meditation? After you've tried to think of some, read what Paul says in 2 Corinthians 5:14 in its context. Does that suggest another benefit to you?

5. This is an ambitious project, but it could benefit you. Choose a modern religion that is considered a cult (you may want to refer to Walter Martin, *The Kingdom of the Cults*). Find out what that religion teaches about Christ—whether he is God and man, or something else. If they teach that he is anything other than God and man, describe how they rob him of his glory.

Moon-like is all other love:
First crescent, then decreasing, gain;
Flower that buds, and soon goes off;
A day that fleets away in rain.

All other love bravely starts out,
But ends with torture, and in tears;
No love can salve the torment out
But that the King of Heaven bears:

For ever springing, ever new,
For ever the full orb, it is
A thing not thinned, from which accrue
Always new sweets, new centuries.

For this love, I all others fled:
Tell me where you may be found![1]

[5]

The River of Love

It is unbought love. . . . You have no cause to boast. He loved you, because he loved you—for nothing. O what a black soul wast thou, when Christ set his love upon thee!
—Robert Murray M'Cheyne

Cur Deus Homo

In the eleventh century, Anselm sat down to explain *Cur Deus Homo*—"Why God Became Man." He wrote for the sake of his brothers and sisters, "that they may be gladdened by understanding and meditating on those things that they believe." His book is now a jewel in the treasury of the church. He masterfully demonstrated how no being except the God-man could atone for our sins and save us.

Anselm showed that the Son of God became man in order to save us because there was no other way. But if we ask

Christ why he became man—not why did he *need* to become man, but why did he *want* to—his answer could be summed up in one word: love.

> The life I live in the body, I live by faith in the Son of God, *who loved me and gave himself for me.* (Galatians 2:20)

> This is how we know what love is: Jesus Christ laid down his life for us. (1 John 3:16)

> To *him who loves us* and has freed us from our sins by his blood, and has made us to be a kingdom and priests to serve his God and Father—to him be glory and power for ever and ever! Amen. (Revelation 1:5–6)

When we gaze on the glory of Christ it's difficult to escape his love. But before we dip our cupped hands into the refreshing river of Christ's love in its glory, let's step upstream and see its headwaters.

THE FOUNTAIN OF LOVE IN ETERNITY

Christ's love for us springs from the Father's eternal love for his people. The Bible returns us to this fountain of love again and again, as the sure source of all our hope and joy. The Father's love is eternally expressed in what he determined to do "before the creation of the world" (Ephesians 1:4), and in how he carried it out by sending his Son (John 3:16). We see the unspeakable love of the God who is Three in One in this: The Father in love determines to save us; the Son in love spills his blood to save us; and the Spirit in love washes us clean with Christ's blood so that we are indeed saved.

> . . . we ought always to thank God for you, brothers loved by the Lord, because from the beginning God chose you to be saved through the sanctifying work of the Spirit and through belief in the truth. (2 Thessalonians 2:13)

> To God's elect . . . who have been chosen according to the foreknowledge of God the Father, through the sanctifying work of the Spirit, for obedience to Jesus Christ and sprinkling by his blood. . . . (1 Peter 1:1–2)

The Father's determination to rescue us is not called love because he loves us "just the way we are." He loved us so much he couldn't leave us the way we were. In fact, his plan included changing us and making us new creatures that would be acceptable to him. But it's called love because of the following reasons:

1. The Father's determination to save us flows from his very nature as Love. "God is love" (1 John 4:8–9). As an eternal act of the will of God, his choosing us can't be caused by anything but who he is, because in eternity there wasn't anything else that could cause his love. And although his determination to save us expresses all his character, it most explicitly expresses his love. Yes, his saving us expresses his righteousness, holiness, wisdom, goodness, truth—everything that he is. But it most especially declares that God is love.

2. The Father's determination to save us was free and undeserved. He chose to love us in eternity—long before we appeared in history. He chose us before there was anything good in us that could excite his love (Romans 9:11). Since we had no way to win his love, the cause of his choosing us must come from within him, not from us. In fact, whatever in us is lovable is a result of his work to save us!

> For he chose us in him before the creation of the world
> to be holy and blameless in his sight. (Ephesians 1:4)

3. The Father's determination to save us set off a chain reaction of unspeakable acts of love. He saves us by multiplied acts of love. Stop and consider the chain of his actions on your behalf to save you. Think of what he did in eternity, determining to save you. Think of the mystery of his wise plan to save through his Son. Think of his preparations to save you, all the groundwork he laid through Israel and the covenants. Think of his willingness to turn his back on his beloved Son, in whom he was well pleased—for your sake. Think of his power in raising Christ from the dead, and seating him at his right hand to pray for you so that you will endure to the end.

> For God so loved the world that he gave his one and
> only Son, that whoever believes in him shall not per-
> ish but have eternal life. (John 3:16)

I have loved you with an everlasting love;
I have drawn you with loving-kindness.
(Jeremiah 31:3)

Praise be to the God and Father of our Lord Jesus Christ, who has blessed us in the heavenly realms with every spiritual blessing in Christ. For he chose us in him before the creation of the world to be holy and blameless in his sight. In love he predestined us to be adopted as his sons through Jesus Christ, in accordance with his pleasure and will. . . . (Ephesians 1:3–6)

Whoever does not love does not know God, because God is love. This is how God showed his love among us: He sent his one and only Son into the world that we might live through him. . . . So we know and rely on the love God has for us. God is love. Whoever lives in love lives in God, and God in him. (1 John 4:8–9, 16)

Don't stop with thoughts of the history of the Father's love as it unfolds in the Scriptures; reflect on how that chain of loving acts extends through your life. Did he show his love to you by bringing you into the world in a Christian home? Did he send a friend into your life at just the right time to bring you to Jesus? Did he reach down to you when you were on the brink of taking your own life? Your testimony of his grace in your life can become an offering of praise to him, and a way to see his glory.

THE RIVER OF LOVE IN HISTORY

Thoughts of the Father's plan to save us are enough to overwhelm our hearts for hours on end. But our goal is to reflect on the glory of Christ, and it is glorious in our eyes that the Father worked all his plans of love through Christ. The Father's love is the fountain and spring, but there's only one stream of that love—and it flows to us through Christ. We would never know the Father's love except through Christ.

To reflect on Christ's love, trace the path of the river of love through history.

At first, all of God's people were made in his image and therefore loved him and were loved by him. All that they were, had, or hoped for sprang from God's goodness and love. Every breath they took was of love to God. It was paradise on earth—a preparation for the eternal life of love in heaven.

By sin they tumbled out of this paradise of love. With a taste of fruit they changed from God's lovers to his enemies. They brought on themselves (and on us) every misery—the sorrows in this life that begin and end, as well as the threat of unending miseries in hell.

While we were in such a wretched state, the first act of love in Christ toward us was pity and compassion. The Scriptures celebrate how our divine Knight hears our cries, the cries of his damsel in distress, and is moved:

> Since the children have flesh and blood, he too shared in their humanity so that by his death he might destroy him who holds the power of death—that is,

the devil—and free those who all their lives were held
in slavery by their fear of death. (Hebrews 2:14–15)

In all their distress *he too was distressed,*
   and the angel of his presence saved them.
In his love and mercy he redeemed them. . . .
       (Isaiah 63:9)

When we had become the apple of his eye, Christ took up
his work for us with inconceivable delight (compare Proverbs
8:30–31). Where did this compassion and delight in him
come from? What drove him who was eternally blessed in his
own self-sufficiency to concern himself with such helpless,
miserable creatures? "He saved us, not because of righteous
things we had done, but because of his mercy" (Titus 3:5).

The Son, eager to save his people, hears from the Father
the way he can save humankind. The road leads through the
darkest heart of difficulties. Of course, no path would slow
the Son *as God;* this plan would be hard, though, because it
demanded that he carry it out in his human nature. The plan
required that the Son would pity us until there was no one
left to pity him when he would need it most. That he would
chase his delight to save us until his own soul was crushed under sorrow. That he would relieve our sufferings by suffering
what we should have suffered. But none of this deterred him
from taking up this work of love and mercy for us. On the
contrary, his love rose to this plan like waves driven by a hur-
ricane. He heard this plan and said, "Here I am—it is written about me in the scroll—I have come to do your will, O
God" (Hebrews 10:7; compare Isaiah 50:5–7).

So the Father prepared a body for him. In this body[2] he was to carry out his mission of love. The Father gave him his humanity just for this, and filled him with immeasurable grace.

Can you see that this glorious love of Christ isn't only the love of a divine person? The Father's love is the love of God. Although this may sound strange, there's something more in the love of Christ. When he loved us he was God *and* man. As a man he shattered every obstacle and loved us to the fullest: He died for us. This is something that God (as God alone) couldn't do.

Now, when we talk about Christ loving us, we can talk about how he loves us as God and how he loves us as man—we can distinguish acts that are human from those that are divine. For example, it was an act of inexpressible love to take on our nature (Hebrews 2:14, 17). Christ did this in his divine nature—he had to, because he did it before he became man. It was another act of his inconceivable love to lay down his life for us (1 John 3:16); yet this was an act of his human nature. But in all of them we're still talking about the love of one person: Jesus Christ. This one person is the God-man; so we can say with the Scriptures that *God* laid down his life for us and purchased the church with his own blood (Acts 20:28).

This love is the glory of Christ. It soars over our heads, beyond the reach of our understanding. But we can adore it by faith.

FIXING HIS LOVE IN YOUR HEART

Even the bit of his love that we can comprehend is marvelous. I hope to stir your heart—and mine—to steadily and patiently reflect on this love.

1. Work to have your mind always ready for such heavenly thoughts. If your thoughts are prisoners of your flesh or can't rise above earthly needs, you won't be able to hold on to a sense of the love of Christ and its glory. High thoughts of his love can't live in the same mind with sewer-dwelling thoughts any more than a mouse can live in the same cage with a boa constrictor. Just as the serpent devours the rodent, a mind mesmerized by worldliness eats up the first feeble attempt to gaze on the Son.

Is your mind fit, as you read the Scriptures quoted in this chapter, to run into the arms of Christ? Or are your thoughts zipping around the world even now?

2. Don't be satisfied with vague notions about the love of Christ. Loose, generic ideas of love won't uncover his glory to your mind. Knowing that Italy is a boot-shaped country in southern Europe will hardly move you; but walk the buzzing, narrow streets of Florence past Dante's house, taste silky gelato from the hand of a laughing vendor, stretch out on the grassy slopes of the Boboli Gardens of the Palazzo Pitti, climb the steps of the Duomo to watch the sun set over the red-gold ribbon of the Arno—and the glory of Italia will stir you!

Relish the finer details of Christ's love: Remember that it's the Lord of glory himself, the Son of God, who loves you. Remember that he loved you so much that he gladly died for you. Spell out for yourself the acts of wisdom, goodness, and grace he showered on you from eternity as God. Recite out loud the pity and compassion he had for you as a man— how his heart was warm toward you (Ephesians 3:19; Hebrews 2:14–15; Revelation 1:5). Let your mind linger over how free his love is, not compelled by anything outside him, and how completely you don't deserve his love (1 John 4:10). In fact, think about what you truly deserved from him, and let that humble your heart and melt it before him.

Last, don't be content to have right thoughts about Christ's love without your heart being moved toward him until you taste his love. If your mind reflects on him but your heart is cold, those sweet thoughts will fade faster than clouds in your coffee. But Christ is meat, bread, food for our souls. Nothing in him nourishes our hearts more than his love; we should always hunger for it.

The love of Christ is glorious. No creature, angel or man, could ever have dreamed the least of it before the Lamb of God came into the world to show his love. And now that he has come, his love towers above our highest and best thoughts, until we gasp in wonder at it.

For Reflection and Discussion

1. Christ is the Bridegroom of the church, his beautiful bride. As his bride, answer the question posed of the beloved in Song of Songs 5:9: "How is your beloved better than others, most beautiful of women?"

2. Explain what is glorious in the fact that Christ alone reveals the Father's love.

3. What do you think of the statement that the Son's love is somehow more than mere divine love, because he is both God and man?

4. Write out, in the form of a prayer of praise, the story of how God saved you. Trace his acts of love in your life

that brought you to saving faith. Be as elaborate and detailed as you can.

5. Make a list of the difficulties and hardships that Jesus had to overcome in his human nature in order to carry out his mission of love for you. Again, be specific. Reading through this list, how does it make you feel toward Christ?

[6]

A Hero to Worship

See, the conquering hero comes!
Sound the trumpets, beat the drums!
—Thomas Morell

What Makes a Hero Glorious?

What makes your favorite hero shine in your eyes? Is it the courage of Indiana Jones swinging down into the snake-filled Well of the Souls? Is it the strength of Superman bringing to a screeching halt a locomotive that is bearing down on Lois and Jimmy? Is it the nobility of Shakespeare's Henry V inspiring his sorely outnumbered troops before the battle of Agincourt? Is it the wits of Sherlock Holmes dogging the trail of arch-villain Moriarty? Or is it the combination of fearlessness, muscle, dignity, and brains in Doc Savage, the consummate superhero?[1]

Whatever heroic traits pop into your mind, I suspect that *obedience* and *suffering* aren't among them. Yet it's in his obedience to God's law and his suffering the curse of that law for us that we see Christ as our conquering hero.

An unseen glory surrounded Christ in all his obedience and suffering. If the rulers of this world had seen it, they wouldn't have crucified the Lord of glory (1 Corinthians 2:8). Yet some saw this glory. They said that they saw "his glory, the glory of the One and Only, who came from the Father" (John 1:14)—and they saw this glory when others saw "no beauty or majesty" in him, "nothing in his appearance" that anyone could desire (Isaiah 53:2). It's the same today. Those who see his glory see it by faith. By faith let's take just a glance in this chapter at the drama of the glory of Christ in his heroic obedience and suffering for us.

Our Hero Conquered by Obedience

What our hero did for us was *obey*. That may not sound heroic, but as we look closely at the nature of his obedience, we'll see its glory.

First, his obedience was free. Think about what it means for us to obey God. Because we're creatures we're obliged to obey him as our Creator. We aren't autonomous—no matter how much our flesh would like us to, we can't simply choose to live outside God's law. But being under this obligation, our obedience can be beautiful when we obey freely, from the heart, without having to be led along by bit and bridle like a stubborn mule (Psalm 32:9). The child who says "I'm

sorry" to his brother only because his father is standing behind him with a belt is not obeying from the heart. There's
no glory in such "obedience."

The situation was different for the Son of God, and it made
his obedience more striking than anything we've done. In the
beginning, before he became a man, he wasn't a creature—he
wasn't naturally subject to the law as we were. In fact, he was the
Lord of the law. But he made a conscious, free choice to subject himself to the law when he said, "Here I am—it is written
about me in the scroll—I have come to do your will, O God"
(Hebrews 10:7). So we can say that Christ obeyed because he
wanted to before he obeyed because he should.

This choice began the glory of his obedience. The wisdom,
grace, love, and humility in this choice animated every act of
his obedience, making it pleasing to God and useful to us.
Christ set out to fulfill the law for others, having no need to fulfill it for himself. For example, when he asked John to baptize
him, John refused at first because he knew Jesus had no sins to
repent of; but Jesus said, "Let it be so now; it is proper for us to
do this to fulfill all righteousness" (Matthew 3:15). For the one
who was Lord of the universe to submit himself to careful, thorough obedience savors of his glorious grace.

Second, his obedience wasn't for him but for us. We
were obliged to obey and couldn't; he wasn't obliged to obey
(except by his free choice) and did. God gave him this
honor: that he should obey for the whole church so that
through his obedience many would be made righteous (Romans 5:19). That the perfect obedience of one man can save
the entire church is glorious.

Third, his obedience perfectly and fully represented the holiness of God in his law. The glory of God's holiness was seen in the law when he wrote the Ten Commandments with his finger in the stone tablets. The glory of his holiness is even more brilliantly displayed when he writes his law on the hearts of believers. But the only complete and perfect example we have is the holiness and obedience of Christ, answering God's commands in every detail.

Fourth, he obeyed in the face of extreme obstacles and opposition. Although he was free from the sinful flesh that remains even in Christians and makes perfect obedience impossible for us, he met more external opposition in temptations, suffering, attacks, and denials than all of us together will ever meet. So the Father says of him, "Although he was a son, he learned obedience from what he suffered" (Hebrews 5:8). He didn't learn how to obey; he learned what it cost to obey. He resisted temptation to the point of shedding his blood—he would rather die a thousand deaths than break the least of God's commands (compare Hebrews 12:1–4).

Fifth, this glory shines brightest when we think about who obeyed God. This was none other than the Son of God made man, God and man in one person. He who was in heaven, above all, Lord of all, at the same time lived in the world as a person of no reputation and walked a path of the strictest obedience to the whole law of God. Godly people prayed to him, yet he prayed himself night and day. All the angels of heaven and all creatures worshiped him, yet he continually carried out all the duties of the worship of God.

He was Lord over the house, yet he diligently observed the lowest office of a servant in the house. He made all men and held them in his hand as clay in the hand of the potter, yet he lived among them as a man and gave every one his due—and beyond that, showed mercy and kindness, giving good things that weren't deserved. This makes the obedience of Christ both mysterious and glorious.

Our Hero Conquered by Suffering

The prophets often describe Christ's work in terms of victory, success, and glorious triumph:

> Who is this coming from Edom,
>> from Bozrah, with his garments stained crimson?
> Who is this, robed in splendor,
>> striding forward in the greatness of his strength?
> "It is I, speaking in righteousness,
>> mighty to save."
> Why are your garments red,
>> like those of one treading the winepress?
> "I have trodden the winepress alone;
>> from the nations no one was with me.
> I trampled them in my anger
>> and trod them down in my wrath;
> their blood spattered my garments,
>> and I stained all my clothing.
> For the day of vengeance was in my heart,
>> and the year of my redemption has come.
> I looked, but there was no one to help,
>> I was appalled that no one gave support;

> so my own arm worked salvation for me,
> and my own wrath sustained me."
> (Isaiah 63:1–5)

But before his exaltation in triumph he had to suffer, as he explained to his disciples on the road to Emmaus: "Did not the Christ have to suffer these things and then enter his glory?" (Luke 24:26; see also Matthew 16:21; Mark 8:31; Luke 9:22; 17:25).

When we begin to consider his sufferings, our minds quickly recoil—we sense that we can't sufficiently conceive how much he must have endured. No one has ever launched into this ocean in meditation without quickly finding himself or herself unable to plumb the depths of it. In this chapter I'll only begin to point at the glory of our Lord's sufferings— the vast part of them will have to stay behind the veil.

Think of your Lord Jesus under the full weight of the wrath of God, under the curse of the law. Think of him taking on the worst that God had ever threatened to sin or sinners. Think of him in his agony and bloody sweat in the Garden of Gethsemane—of his loud cries and prayers when he was sorrowful to the point of death, as he began to be amazed at the things that were coming on him.[2] Think of him in battle against all the powers of darkness, and the rage and madness of men. Think of him suffering in body and soul. Think of him losing his name, his reputation, his goods, his life. Some of these sufferings came immediately from God above; others from devils and wicked men acting according to God's wise plan. Think of him praying, weeping, crying out, bleeding, dying—in all this making his soul an offering for sin.

By oppression and judgment he was taken away.
   And who can speak of his descendants?
For he was cut off from the land of the living;
   for the transgression of my people he was stricken.
        (Isaiah 53:8)

I'll leave you to explore Christ's sufferings yourself, until you're overwhelmed with holy admiration for him.

What is man that you are mindful of him,
   the son of man that you care for him?
        (Psalm 8:4)

Who has understood the mind of the LORD,
   or instructed him as his counselor?
        (Isaiah 40:13)

Oh, the depth of the riches of the wisdom and
      knowledge of God!
   How unsearchable his judgments,
   and his paths beyond tracing out!
        (Romans 11:33)

What can we say in response to this? God didn't withhold his only Son, but gave him up to death and these evils for us poor, lost sinners. For our sakes the eternal Son of God submitted himself to all the evils that our sins deserved so that we might be delivered from death and all these evils!

Isn't this suffering Lamb glorious in your eyes?

When Adam had sinned and eternally ruined himself

and all his descendants, he stood ashamed, afraid, trembling, as one ready to perish forever, under the frown of God. He deserved death, and he expected to die immediately. As he stood there trembling, the Lord Jesus came to him in the promise and said, as it were,

> Poor creature! How miserable you are! How wretched you have become! What happened to the beauty, the glory of that image of God in which you were created? How is it that you've taken on the monstrous shape and image of Satan? And yet your present misery is nothing compared with what's to come: eternal torment lies at your door. But look up once more—look to me, that you may have some glimpse of what is in the designs of infinite wisdom, love, and grace. Come out of your silly hiding place. I'll put myself in your mess. I'll bear the burden of guilt and punishment that would sink you eternally into the bottom of hell. I'll repay that which I never took, and be made a curse for you, that you might be blessed forever.

He says the same to us as sinners, and invites us to come to him.

Adoring the Slain Lamb

Before our very eyes Jesus Christ has been clearly portrayed as crucified (Galatians 3:1). So let's gaze on him in wonder as poor, despised, persecuted, reproached, reviled, and hanged on a tree. And remember that while he's facing such an onslaught from outside, he knows and feels in his heart the full wrath of God against our sins. But why is his misery recorded for us so clearly in the gospel, and so often preached to us from the pulpit? What glory is there in such suffering? Aren't these the very things that Jews and Gentiles stumbled and took offense at (1 Corinthians 1:23)? Doesn't it seem to the world that we're fools to look for help from the miseries of Christ? To look for life by his death?

Such is the wisdom of the world. But to us who believe, even the sufferings of our Lord are honorable, glorious, and precious—we even see in his sufferings the wisdom and power of God:

> For in Scripture it says:
>
> "See, I lay a stone in Zion,
>   a chosen and precious cornerstone,
> and the one who trusts in him
>   will never be put to shame."
>
> Now to you who believe, this stone is precious. But to those who do not believe,
>
> "The stone the builders rejected
>   has become the capstone,"
>
> and,
>
> "A stone that causes men to stumble
>   and a rock that makes them fall."

They stumble because they disobey the message—which is also what they were destined for.

But you are a chosen people, a royal priesthood, a holy nation, a people belonging to God, that you may declare the praises of him who called you out of darkness into his wonderful light. (1 Peter 2:6–9)

We preach Christ crucified: a stumbling block to Jews and foolishness to Gentiles, but to those whom God has called, both Jews and Greeks, Christ the power of God and the wisdom of God. For the foolishness of God is wiser than man's wisdom, and the weakness of God is stronger than man's strength. (1 Corinthians 1:23–25)

God has made his light shine in the darkness of our hearts, and has opened our eyes to see his wisdom and power in Christ crucified. So we have new eyes, eyes of faith that can see Christ whipped and bleeding, and see him as our hero. By faith we know that by those bloody stripes we're healed (Isaiah 53:5; 1 Peter 2:24). And by faith we enter heaven and join around the throne of the slain Lamb:

Then I saw a Lamb, looking as if it had been slain, standing in the center of the throne, encircled by the four living creatures and the elders. He had seven horns and seven eyes, which are the seven spirits of God sent out into all the earth. He came and took the scroll from the right hand of him who sat on the throne. And when he had taken it, the four living creatures and the twenty-four elders fell down before the Lamb. Each one had a harp and they were holding golden bowls full of incense, which are the prayers of the saints. And they sang a new song:

"You are worthy to take the scroll
    and to open its seals,
because you were slain,
        and with your blood you purchased men for God
        from every tribe and language and people and
            nation.
You have made them to be a kingdom and priests
            to serve our God,
        and they will reign on the earth."

Then I looked and heard the voice of many angels, numbering thousands upon thousands, and ten thousand times ten thousand. They encircled the throne and the living creatures and the elders. In a loud voice they sang:

"Worthy is the Lamb, who was slain,
to receive power and wealth and wisdom and
            strength
and honor and glory and praise!"

Then I heard every creature in heaven and on earth and under the earth and on the sea, and all that is in them, singing:

"To him who sits on the throne and to the Lamb
be praise and honor and glory and power,
for ever and ever!"

The four living creatures said, "Amen," and the elders fell down and worshiped. (Revelation 5:6–14)

For Reflection and Discussion

1. Christ is the Bridegroom of the church, his beautiful bride. As his bride, answer the question posed of the beloved in Song of Songs 5:9: "How is your beloved better than others, most beautiful of women?"

2. How do you define "heroic"?

3. What is heroic about Christ's obedience?

4. What is heroic about Christ's suffering?

5. Make a list of things in Christ's life that would have been obstacles that he had to overcome as a man in order to obey God.

6. Choose a passage of Scripture that speaks of the sufferings of our Lord (such as Isaiah 52:13–53:12; Matthew 26:36–46; or Matthew 27:27–56). After meditating on these verses, write a six- to seven-sentence prayer of praise to Christ for these sufferings. Use details from the Scripture passage to make your prayer specific—tell him exactly what you admire about him.

7. George Herbert wrote a poem called "The Sacrifice" that meditates deeply on Christ's suffering. The narrator of the poem is Christ—he relates through his eyes many of the things that broke his heart in the days lead-

ing up to and including his murder. I've included the poem after this chapter. Please set aside a day or two of your secret prayers to work through this before Christ, adoring him for all he did for you.

The Sacrifice[3]

Oh all ye, who pass by, whose eyes and mind
To worldly things are sharp, but to me blind;
To me, who took eyes that I might you find:
     Was ever grief like mine?

The princes of my people make a head
Against their Maker: they do wish me dead,
Who cannot wish, except I give them bread;
     Was ever grief like mine?

Without me each one, who doth now me brave,
Had to this day been an Egyptian slave.
They use that power against me, which I gave:
     Was ever grief like mine?

Mine own apostle, who the bag did bear,
Though he had all I had, did not forbear
To sell me also, and to put me there:
     Was ever grief like mine?

For thirty pence he did my death devise,
Who at three hundred did the ointment prize,
Not half so sweet as my sweet sacrifice:
     Was ever grief like mine?

Therefore my soul melts, and my heart's dear treas-
     ure
Drops blood (the only beads) my words to measure:

O let this cup pass, if it be thy pleasure:
      Was ever grief like mine?

These drops being tempered with a sinner's tears
A balsam are for both the hemispheres:
Curing all wounds, but mine; all, but my fears:
      Was ever grief like mine?

Yet my disciples sleep; I cannot gain
One hour of watching; but their drowsy brain
Comforts not me, and doth my doctrine stain:
      Was ever grief like mine?

Arise, arise, they come. Look how they run!
Alas! what haste they make to be undone!
How with their lanterns do they seek the sun!
      Was ever grief like mine?

With clubs and staves they seek me, as a thief,
Who am the Way and Truth, the true relief;
Most true to those, who are my greatest grief:
      Was ever grief like mine?

Judas, dost thou betray me with a kiss?
Canst thou find hell about my lips? and miss
Of life, just at the gates of life and bliss?
      Was ever grief like mine?

See, they lay hold on me, not with the hands
Of faith, but fury: yet at their commands

I suffer binding, who have loosed their bands:
Was ever grief like mine?

All my disciples fly; fear puts a bar
Betwixt my friends and me. They leave the star,
That brought the wise men of the East from far.
Was ever grief like mine?

Then from one ruler to another bound
They lead me; urging, that it was not sound
What I taught: comments would the test confound.
Was ever grief like mine?

The priest and rulers all false witness seek
'Gainst him, who seeks not life, but is the meek
And ready Paschal Lamb of this great week:
Was ever grief like mine?

Then they accuse me of great blasphemy,
That I did thrust into the Deity,
Who never thought that any robbery:
Was ever grief like mine?

Some said, that I the Temple to the floor
In three days razed, and raisèd as before.
Why, he that built the world can do much more:
Was ever grief like mine?

Then they condemn me all with that same breath,
Which I do give them daily, unto death.

Thus Adam my first breathing rendereth:
        Was ever grief like mine?

They bind, and lead me unto Herod: he
Sends me to Pilate. This makes them agree;
But yet their friendship is my enmity:
        Was ever grief like mine?

Herod and all his bands do set me light,
Who teach all hands to war, fingers to fight,
And only am the Lord of Hosts and might:
        Was ever grief like mine?

Herod in judgement sits, while I do stand;
Examines me with a censorious hand:
I him obey, who all things else command:
        Was ever grief like mine?

The Jews accuse me with dispitefulnesse;
And vying malice with my gentleness,
Pick quarrels with their only happiness:
        Was ever grief like mine?

I answer nothing, but with patience prove
If stony hearts will melt with gentle love.
But who does hawk at eagles with a dove?
        Was ever grief like mine?

My silence rather doth augment their cry;
My dove doth back into my bosom fly,

Because the raging waters still are high:
        Was ever grief like mine?

Heark how they cry aloud still, *Crucify:*
It is not fit he live a day, they cry,
Who cannot live less than eternally:
        Was ever grief like mine?

Pilate, a stranger, holdeth off; but they,
Mine own dear people, cry, *Away, away,*
With noises confusèd frighting the day:
        Was ever grief like mine?

Yet still they shout, and cry, and stop their ears,
Putting my life among their sins and fears,
And therefore wish *my blood on them and theirs:*
        Was ever grief like mine?

See how spite cankers things. These words aright
Usèd, and wishèd, are the whole world's light:
But honey is their gall, brightness their night:
        Was ever grief like mine?

They choose a murderer, and all agree
In him to do themselves a courtesy:
For it was their own case who killèd me:
        Was ever grief like mine?

And a seditious murderer he was:
But I the Prince of peace; peace that doth pass

All understanding, more then heav'n doth glass:
       Was ever grief like mine?

Why, Caesar is their only king, not I:
He clave the stone rock, when they were dry;
But surely not their hearts, as I well try:
       Was ever grief like mine?

Ah! how they scourge me! yet my tenderness
Doubles each lash: and yet their bitterness
Winds up my grief to a mysteriousness:
       Was ever grief like mine?

They buffet him, and box him as they list,
Who grasps the earth and heaven with his fist,
And never yet, whom he would punish, missed:
       Was ever grief like mine?

Behold, they spit on me in scornful wise,
Who by my spittle gave the blind man eyes,
Leaving his blindness to my enemies:
       Was ever grief like mine?

My face they cover, though it be divine.
As Moses' face was veilèd, so is mine,
Lest on their double-dark souls either shine:
       Was ever grief like mine?

Servants and abjects flout me; they are witty:
Now prophesy who strikes thee, is their ditty.

So they in me deny themselves all pity:
            Was ever grief like mine?

And now I am delivered unto death,
Which each one calls for so with utmost breath,
That he before me well nigh suffereth:
            Was ever grief like mine?

Weep not, dear friends, since I for both have wept
When all my tears were blood, the while you slept:
Your tears for your own fortunes should be kept:
            Was ever grief like mine?

The soldiers lead me to the common hall;
There they deride me, they abuse me all:
Yet for twelve heav'nly legions I could call:
            Was ever grief like mine?

Then with a scarlet robe they me array;
Which shows my blood to be the only way
And cordial left to repair man's decay:
            Was ever grief like mine?

Then on my head a crown of thorns I wear:
For these are all the grapes Sion doth bear,
Though I my vine planted and watered there:
            Was ever grief like mine?

So sits the earth's great curse in Adam's fall
Upon my head: so I remove it all

From th' earth unto my brows, and bear the thrall:
    Was ever grief like mine?

Then with the recd they gave to me before,
They strike my head, the rock from thence all store
Of heav'nly blessings issue evermore:
    Was ever grief like mine?

They bow their knees to me, and cry, *Hail king*:
Whatever scoffs and scornfulness can bring,
I am the floor, the sink, where they it fling:
    Was ever grief like mine?

Yet since man's scepters are as frail as reeds,
And thorny all their crowns, bloody their weeds;
I, who am Truth, turn into truth their deeds:
    Was ever grief like mine?

The soldiers also spit upon that face,
Which angels did desire to have the grace,
And prophets, once to see, but found no place:
    Was ever grief like mine?

Thus trimmèd, forth they bring me to the rout,
Who *Crucify him*, cry with one strong shout.
God holds his peace at man, and man cries out:
    Was ever grief like mine?

They lead me in once more, and putting then
Mine own clothes on, they lead me out again.

Whom devils fly, thus is he tossed of men:
                    Was ever grief like mine?

And now weary of sport, glad to engross
All spite in one, counting my life their loss,
They carry me to my most bitter cross:
                    Was ever grief like mine?

O all ye who passe by, behold and see,
Man stole the fruit, but I must climb the tree;
The tree of life to all, but only me:
                    Was ever grief like mine?

Lo, here I hang, charged with a world of sin,
The greater world o' th' two; for that came in
By words, but this by sorrow I must win:
                    Was ever grief like mine?

Such sorrow as, if sinful man could feel,
Or feel his part, he would not cease to kneel.
Till all were melted, though he were all steel:
                    Was ever grief like mine?

But, *O my God, my God!* why leav'st thou me,
The son, in whom thou dost delight to be?
My God, my God—
                    Never was grief like mine.

Shame tears my soul, my body many a wound;
Sharp nails pierce this, but sharper that confound;

Reproaches, which are free, while I am bound.
          Was ever grief like mine?

Now heal thy self, physician; now come down.
Alas! I did so, when I left my crown
And father's smile for you, to feel his frown:
          Was ever grief like mine?

In healing not my self, there doth consist
All that salvation, which ye now resist;
Your safety in my sickness doth subsist:
          Was ever grief like mine?

Betwixt two thieves I spend my utmost breath,
As he that for some robbery suffereth.
Alas! what have I stolen from you? Death.
          Was ever grief like mine?

A king my title is, prefixed on high;
Yet by my subjects am condemned to die
A servile death in servile company:
          Was ever grief like mine?

They give me vinegar mingled with gall,
But more with malice: yet, when they did call,
With manna, angels' food, I fed them all:
          Was ever grief like mine?

They part my garments, and by lot dispose
My coat, the type of love, which once cured those

Who sought for help, never malicious foes:
  Was ever grief like mine?

Nay, after death their spite shall further go;
For they will pierce my side, I full well know;
That as sin came, so Sacraments might flow:
  Was ever grief like mine?

But now I die; now all is finishèd.
My woe, man's weal: and now I bow my head.
Only let others say, when I am dead,
  Never was grief like mine.

      (George Herbert)

[7]

God's Right-Hand Man

. . . every wretch, pining and pale before,
Beholding him, plucks comfort from his looks.
—Shakespeare[1]

A KING IN A CLOAK

It's 3:00 in the morning before the battle at Agincourt. The campfires of both the French and the English can be seen burning in the night, and the sounds of hammers on armor "give dreadful note of preparation." The French are like crowing roosters in their confidence, while the grossly outnumbered English stare at the moon like "so many horrid ghosts."

In Shakespeare's version of the history of Henry V, the king takes the cloak of old Sir Thomas Erpingham and walks among his men. In the darkness and under the hood of the cloak, no one recognizes King Harry. As you can imagine, this changes the tone of the conversations he has. He ends up sitting around a fire with John Bates, Alexander Court, and Michael Williams, debating whether their conflict with the French is just, and what responsibility the soldiers have if they fight at the king's command. Williams takes exception to something the king says and rebukes him (not knowing he's the king!).

KING HARRY: Your reproof is something too round. I should be angry with you, if the time were convenient.

WILLIAMS: Let it be a quarrel between us, if you live.

KING HARRY: I embrace it.

WILLIAMS: How shall I know thee again?

KING HARRY: Give me any gage of thine, and I will wear it in my bonnet. Then if ever thou darest acknowledge it, I will make it my quarrel.

WILLIAMS: Here's my glove. Give me another of thine.

KING HARRY: There.

They exchange gloves.

WILLIAMS: This will I also wear in my cap. If ever thou come to me and say, after tomorrow, 'This is my glove', by this hand I will take thee a box on the ear.

KING HARRY: If ever I live to see it, I will challenge it.

WILLIAMS: Thou darest as well be hanged.

KING HARRY: Well, I will do it, though I take thee in the King's company.[2]

Shakespeare's irony is rich. This is a quarrel that could never have happened if the king appeared to Williams in his purple robes and wearing his crown, with his retinue surrounding him. Williams would never have threatened to box the ears of his lord and sovereign!

ANOTHER KING, ANOTHER CLOAK

If the rulers of this age had known that the man Jesus was the King of all under the cloak of his human flesh, "they would not have crucified the Lord of glory" (1 Corinthians 2:8). None of the sufferings of Christ that we surveyed in the previous chapter would have been possible if he hadn't hidden his royal glory under the cloak of the Man of Sorrows. But after his suffering was finished on the cross, the cloak was ripped away: He rose from the dead and ascended to heaven to take his rightful place at the right hand of the Majesty on high. Theologians call this his *exaltation*. It's the revelation, or unveiling, or "uncloaking" of his glory.

Everything the Old Testament prophets predicted about Christ pointed either to his suffering or to this exaltation:

> Concerning this salvation, the prophets, who spoke of the grace that was to come to you, searched intently and with the greatest care, trying to find out the time and circumstances to which the Spirit of Christ in them was pointing when he predicted the *sufferings* of Christ and the *glories* that would follow. (1 Peter 1:10–11)

So when Christ opened the Scriptures to two disciples on the road to Emmaus, he began by saying, "Did not the Christ have to suffer these things and then enter his glory?" (Luke 24:26). Paul also sings this chorus of Christ's sufferings followed by his glory:

> Your attitude should be the same as that of Christ Jesus:

> Who, being in very nature God,
>   did not consider equality with God something to
>   be grasped,
> but made himself nothing,
>   taking the very nature of a servant,
>   being made in human likeness.
> And being found in appearance as a man,
>   he humbled himself
>   and became obedient to death—
>   even death on a cross!
> *Therefore God exalted him to the highest place*
>   *and gave him the name that is above every name,*
> *that at the name of Jesus every knee should bow,*
>   *in heaven and on earth and under the earth,*
> *and every tongue confess that Jesus Christ is Lord,*
>   *to the glory of God the Father.*
>   (Philippians 2:5–11)

If we want to know Christ as he is revealed in the Scriptures, we have to understand his sufferings—but we also have to know him in his exaltation.

OUR OWN SUFFERING AND GLORY

In fact, we need to know both the suffering and the exaltation of the Lamb. By reflecting on both, we'll "pluck comfort from his looks." And we'll need that comfort, because the pattern of "first suffering, then glory" isn't only for Christ, but for us:

> Here is a trustworthy saying:
>
> If we died with him,
>   we will also live with him;
> if we endure,
>   we will also reign with him.
>   (2 Timothy 2:11–12)

It took great courage for Christ to endure his sufferings. He faced them because he knew what lay before him—an unspeakable joy that would be his reward (Hebrews 12:2). For us to meet our suffering and not give up we must look at our Lord, admire his courage, revel in his exaltation—and seeing him in his glory will ennoble our faith. We'll be carried through our hardships by the certainty that we, too, will share his glory and joy, as he has promised.

> Let us fix our eyes on Jesus, the author and perfecter of our faith, who for the joy set before him endured the cross, scorning its shame, and sat down at the right hand of the throne of God. Consider him who endured such opposition from sinful men, so that you will not grow weary and lose heart. (Hebrews 12:2–3)

The Lamb of God won our salvation by his suffering and his exaltation. Without these two there would be no church. If he hadn't suffered, our sins wouldn't have been paid for. If he hadn't been exalted, we wouldn't have known whether God had accepted his sacrifice, or that he had defeated death—and we wouldn't know whether we would be exalted with him.

But he was exalted indeed!

SEEING THE SON OF MAN AT THE RIGHT HAND OF GOD

Christ prayed in John 17:24 for us to be with him and see his glory. The particular glory he wanted us to see was his exaltation at the right hand of the Father. It wasn't the only glory he wanted us to see, but his exaltation is the way all of his glories are magnified before our eyes. All the glory of Christ that we've looked at so far was under a cloak while he was in the world. But in his exaltation the cloak is ripped away so that we can see the wonder of who he is and all he did. And when he appears and we see him as he is (1 John 3:2), what we'll see is this exalted glory. It was the glory that the Father granted to him before the foundation of the world (John 17:5, 24) and that was poured out on him when he ascended to heaven to sit at the right hand of God (Luke 22:69; Acts 2:33; Hebrews 1:3).

But don't make the mistake of thinking that the glory of his exaltation is the glory of his *becoming* God. He had always been God and could not *not* be God. The glory of his deity was hidden under the cloak of his humanity while he was in the world, but when he rose from the dead he was "declared with power to be the Son of God by his resurrection from the dead" (Romans 1:4). This *declaration* of his glory is called his exaltation.

A total eclipse doesn't reduce by a single photon the natural beauty, light, and glory of the sun. To us on earth it looks like a dark, lifeless meteor; but when it moves out from behind the moon, it again shines with its natural light and glory. It was the same with the divine nature of Christ as it was "eclipsed" when he took the "nature of a servant" (Philippians 2:7), a poor and despised man in this world. But the eclipse is over. His glory now shines in its infinite luster and beauty. And when those who knew him here as a "man of sorrows" saw him in all the boundless glory of the divine nature, their souls burst with joy and admiration. This is one reason he prayed for them to be with him and to see his glory; for he knew what unspeakable satisfaction it would be to them forever.

THE GLORY OF CHRIST'S EXALTATION

Many masters have tried to paint the scene of the Lamb on the throne, at the right hand of the Father. But how can we begin to imagine the splendor of this scene? Paint all the gold crowns you like; make the light streaming from Christ as bright as you can; surround him with crowds of men and angels stretching into the infinite distance. As stunning as such a picture might be under the brush of Michelangelo or Giotto or Rembrandt or Van Eyck, it will be pale as a smoggy sky over L.A. compared to what we'll see on the Day of Christ's glory.

Likewise, my words can't begin to touch the true glory of the exalted Lamb. How can I describe the exaltation of the Lamb of God? He is exalted over the whole creation in power, dignity, authority, and rule. Not just as God, but as man, he rules the universe. Speaking of Christ, Paul says,

> For by him all things were created: things in heaven and on earth, visible and invisible, whether thrones or powers or rulers or authorities; all things were created by him and for him. (Colossians 1:16)

He is exalted by the love and approval of the Father. The Father delights in his Son and is so pleased with his work as Mediator that he has given him the seat of honor at his right hand. There's only one seat at the right hand of the Majesty on high—and that seat was reserved for no other creature. It is an unparalleled honor.

> The Son is the radiance of God's glory and the exact representation of his being, sustaining all things by his powerful word. After he had provided purification for sins, he sat down at the right hand of the Majesty in heaven. So he became as much superior to the angels as the name he has inherited is superior to theirs. (Hebrews 1:3–4)

His exaltation fully and finally uncovers and broadcasts his divine wisdom, love, and grace in his work to redeem his bride, the church. Again, no angels or men share one bit of his glory. Because we can see it here only by faith, we see it vaguely as in an old looking glass; but in heaven it radiates in its brightness, to the unending joy of all who see him.

Then I looked and heard the voice of many angels, numbering thousands upon thousands, and ten
thousand times ten thousand. They encircled the
throne and the living creatures and the elders. In a
loud voice they sang:

"Worthy is the Lamb, who was slain,
to receive power and wealth and wisdom and
      strength
and honor and glory and praise!"
      (Revelation 5:11–12)

SEEING THE EXALTED CHRIST

Since we're on earth, how can we see the exalted glory
of Christ on his throne in heaven? Once again, the only way
is by faith—faith clinging to God's revelation of the glory of
Christ in his Word, faith constantly reflecting and meditating on his wisdom and love and sufferings and exaltation.
This is the exercise for our faith that strengthens it; this is
the food for our faith that makes it flourish.

But what do we tend to fix our minds on? Where do our
minds run when they're free from the duties of work and
school? I confess that my mind is ready to sprint from one
end of the earth to the other, but slow to lift a sleepy eye to
the heavens. If I weren't fretting about my bank balance,
scheming how to get to Paris for my next vacation, or stew-
ing about what someone at work said someone else at work
said about me, I don't know what my mind would do!

What if I put aside all those thoughts about me, me, me,
and thought for a moment about Christ seated at the right

hand of the Majesty on high? What if I memorized passages from Colossians and Hebrews and Romans, and reflected on what it means for all the creatures of heaven and earth to bow before this man who hung on a cross for me? Or if I considered that this exalted One, who is loved and approved by the Father, is the very One who said that he wants me to be with him where he is (John 14:3; 17:24)? What keeps me from such delicious meditations?

Is it that I'm satisfied that eternity will be enough to adore him—that I can wait until heaven before I gaze on his glory? Am I so crass to think that I'm saved and sealed, so why bother making any extraordinary effort? But if I don't have any taste for the glory of Christ now, what makes me think I'll develop an appetite for it in heaven?

Isn't it part of faith that we prefer Christ above ourselves? That we rest in his works of righteousness rather than our own, and his suffering in our place? Then faith, if true to Christ and not just a figment of the imagination, should easily give up thoughts of self in exchange for thoughts of the Lamb.

Do you need something to draw you toward reflections on Christ? Think about it: Who is it that is exalted over all? Who is surrounded by glory, majesty, and power? Who is enthroned at the right hand of the Majesty on high, resting his feet on all his enemies? Isn't it he who in this world was poor, despised, persecuted, and slain—all for your sake? Isn't it the same Jesus who loved us, and gave himself for us, and washed us in his own blood? So Peter told the Jews that the same Jesus whom they slew and hanged on a tree, "God exalted . . . to his own right hand as Prince and Savior that he might give repentance and forgiveness of sins to Israel" (Acts 5:30–31). If we value his love at all, if we care in the least what he did and suffered for his church, we can't help but rejoice in his glory.

> *Blessed Jesus! We can add nothing to you, nothing to your glory. But it is joy deep in our hearts that you are what you are—that you are so gloriously exalted at the right hand of God. We long to behold your glory more fully and clearly, as you prayed and promised. Amen.*

FOR REFLECTION AND DISCUSSION

1. Christ is the Bridegroom of the church, his beautiful bride. As his bride, answer the question posed of the beloved in Song of Songs 5:9: "How is your beloved better than others, most beautiful of women?"

2. What do you think it means that Christ was "exalted to the right hand of God" (Acts 2:33)? Why did God exalt him? What does it mean that he is at God's right hand?

3. Do you think it's true that meditating on Christ in his suffering and exaltation can comfort you and give you hope in your own suffering? If so, how?

4. Pick a passage of Scripture that describes the exalted Christ (such as Psalm 110; Colossians 1:15–29; Hebrews 1; Revelation 4 or 5). Make it your meditation every day this week—memorize it, if you can. At the end of the week write your own six- to seven-sentence prayer of praise to Christ, focusing on details of his exaltation and your response to it.

[8]

The Center of the Old Testament

Ex umbris et imaginibus in veritatem.
From shadows and types to reality.
—Cardinal Newman

A MASTER TEACHER

I must have looked like a zombie from *The Night of the Living Dead* as I walked back to my apartment for lunch every day. It was my first semester at seminary, and my head was spinning out of control. I would open the door, plop into our old gray recliner, and stare with glassy eyes into infinity. But my blank expression didn't come from unconsciousness. *Au contraire!* My mind was reeling with wondrous thoughts, ideas, perspectives, implications.

The last class before lunch was an introduction to the

historical books of the Old Testament. Every day I saw something new—I saw the significance and relevance of passages and stories that had until then been to me at best some inspiring tales, and at worst dark and closed. And I was learning how to mine my own treasures from them, with new tools and the skills to use them.

Some people might think that the class was great because we were, after all, studying the Bible. But I had lots of other Bible classes that year, and none of them affected me the way that one did. The difference was the teacher, Richard Pratt. He knew what to teach (and what to leave to the textbooks), and how to teach in a way that made me want to learn. He didn't just show me new things, but he showed me how to see old things in a new way that made better sense. And he didn't just show me things in a new way, but gave me glasses so that I could see things in a new way long after I left the classroom. Richard Pratt was a master teacher—and whether you're studying the Scriptures or quantum physics or how to rebuild an engine, a master teacher makes all the difference in the world.

Didn't Our Hearts Burn?

What would you give to have been with Cleopas and the other disciple as they walked with "their faces downcast" on the road to Emmaus (Luke 24:13–32)? They were confused and discouraged, because they had known Jesus as "a prophet, powerful in word and deed before God and all the people" (verse 19) and "had hoped that he was the one who was going to redeem Israel" (verse 21); but "the chief priests and . . . rulers handed him over to be sentenced to death, and they crucified him" (verse 20). As these two hang-dog disciples walked along trying to figure all this out, they were joined by someone they didn't recognize (verse 16). As he joined their conversation, they were amazed that he seemed to know none of the latest news of Jesus of Nazareth and what had happened in the past few days (verse 18). But then the stranger turned the conversation and their entire world upside down: "He said to them, 'How foolish you are, and how slow of heart to believe all that the prophets have spoken! Did not the Christ have to suffer these things and then enter his glory?' And beginning with Moses and all the Prophets, he explained to them what was said in all the Scriptures concerning himself" (verses 25–27).

Later this intriguing stranger sat down to dinner with them. He broke the bread, and instantly they recognized him—their new teacher was in fact their old teacher. It was Jesus, the Master, raised from the dead! In a heartbeat he disappeared (verses 28–31). I imagine they were breathless, their minds spinning out of control, as they turned to each other and said, "Were not our hearts burning within us while he talked with us on the road and opened the Scriptures to us?" (verse 32).

How I would love to have been there! Jesus was the Master of master teachers, and he unfolded to them the wonderful mystery of how he, the Christ, was the subject of the entire Old Testament. He began with Moses—the first five books of the Bible—and traced what was said about him all the way through the Prophets. In other words, he showed them how the Old Testament from beginning to end told of the Christ.

Christ is the line of life and light that runs through the whole Old Testament. Only by seeing him in its pages can we rightly grasp the Old Testament. If we neglect to look for him there, we'll be as blind in reading it as are the unbelieving Jews, who read with a veil over their minds. Only faith, discovering the glory of Christ, can remove that veil of darkness (2 Corinthians 3:14–16). So let's look briefly at some of the ways that the glory of Christ was represented to believers in the Old Testament.

CHRIST THE GLORIOUS TABERNACLE

Do you know the name of the first person in the Bible who is referred to as being "full of the Holy Spirit"? Here's a hint: He is first mentioned in Exodus 31. Give up? Bezalel son of Uri, of course!

> Then the LORD said to Moses, "See, I have chosen Bezalel son of Uri, the son of Hur, of the tribe of Judah, and I have filled him with the Spirit of God, with skill, ability and knowledge in all kinds of crafts—to make artistic designs for work in gold, silver and bronze, to cut and set stones, to work in wood, and to engage in all kinds of craftsmanship. Moreover, I have appointed Oholiab son of Ahisamach, of the tribe of Dan, to help him. Also I have given skill to all the craftsmen to make everything I have commanded you: the Tent of Meeting, the ark of the Testimony with the atonement cover on it, and all the other furnishings of the tent—the table and its articles, the pure gold lampstand and

all its accessories, the altar of incense, the altar of burnt offering and all its utensils, the basin with its stand—and also the woven garments, both the sacred garments for Aaron the priest and the garments for his sons when they serve as priests, and the anointing oil and fragrant incense for the Holy Place. They are to make them just as I commanded you." (Exodus 31:1–11)

The ceremonies of worship in the Old Testament were complex, beautiful, and mysterious. They were designed by God's wisdom and so important to him that he filled an artist with his Spirit in order to make the objects that would be used to perform the ceremonies. These forms of worship became the center of Israel's life because it was through them that God showed his people the glory of the Christ to come.

What were the tabernacle and temple? What were the Holy Place and its utensils? What were the oracle, the ark, the cherubim, the mercy seat? What was the high priest in all his vestments and duties? What were the sacrifices and annual sprinkling of blood in the Most Holy Place? What was the whole system of their worship ceremonies? Were they anything but representations of Christ in his glory as God and man, and his glory as our Mediator and Redeemer? They were a shadow, and the body that cast the shadow was Christ (see Hebrews 8 and 9).

Before we try to see Christ's glory in the ceremonies and instruments of worship in the Old Testament, we need some encouragement to help us get over our fears of symbolism:

We in the West aren't very much at ease with symbolism ourselves. We live in an industrialized society dominated by scientific and technological forms of knowledge. Such knowledge minimizes the play of metaphors and the personal depth dimensions of human living. For many people, "real" truth means technological truth, that is, truth swept free of metaphor and symbolism. We meet symbolism mostly in advertising, and such use of symbolism rouses our suspicions and often ends by producing indifference.

I am convinced that God does not share our general cultural aversion to metaphors and symbols. He wrote the Old Testament, which contains a good deal of poetry and many uses of metaphor. . . . We must adapt to the fact that symbols and metaphors can speak truly and powerfully without speaking with pedantic scientific precision. A symbol may suggests a deep truth or even a cluster of related truths without blurting everything out in plain talk and making everything crystal clear. An element of mystery may remain, because a symbol can suggest a whole host of connections.[1]

In other words, this exercise of reflecting on the glory of the Lamb of God as it's pictured in Israel's worship might leave us not only confused and tentative, but even a bit skeptical. But if I read the Book of Hebrews (and the rest of the New Testament) right, the problem is ours. So I recommend that you find a solid commentator (such as Poythress)[2] to help start you on the path of seeing Christ in the tabernacle.

For example, let's look at Christ in two pieces of tabernacle furniture.

The perpetual light of the lampstand in the Holy Place pointed to the true Light that was coming into the world (Exodus 27:20–21; Leviticus 24:1–4). The lamp was continually filled with oil (as Christ was continually full of the Spirit) so that it would light up the tabernacle day and night. It reminded worshipers of God their Creator and Redeemer. As Creator he made the light shine out of the darkness, and as Redeemer he was the pillar of fire by night that led them out of Egypt and through the wilderness to the Promised Land. This imagery points to Christ who is our Creator and Redeemer (Colossians 1:15–20), who is the light that shines in our dark souls to recreate us (2 Corinthians 4:6), and the true light that shines through spiritual darkness to make the blind see (John 1:5, 9; 8:12; 9:3–6).

We could go farther with the lampstand and its imagery—we could talk about its shape as a tree with branches and almond flowers, and see Christ as the Tree of Life and the fruitfulness of his light giving new life to the world. But these few suggestions are only meant to prime the pump of your own reflection on Christ.

The bread of the presence pointed to the true Bread that was coming down from heaven (Exodus 25:23–30). This bread was a delightful symbol of God as the host of a meal, and the worshipers as his honored guests whom he would feed and protect. It reminded them of the manna and its sweet taste, a symbol of the goodness of God and of his daily provision, since he gave the manna to them day after day in the wilderness. Jesus made it plain that he was the substance behind the shadow:

> I tell you the truth, it is not Moses who has given you the bread from heaven, but it is my Father who gives you the true bread from heaven. For the bread of God is he who comes down from heaven and gives life to the world. . . . I am the bread of life. He who comes to me will never go hungry, and he who believes in me will never be thirsty. (John 6:32–33, 35)

Take these few suggestive paragraphs as your starting point, and look for Christ in the worship of the Old Testament. Let the New Testament guide you into the richness of the imagery.[3] The sum is, "Moses was faithful as a servant in all God's house, testifying to what would be said in the future" (Hebrews 3:5). All that Moses did when he built the tabernacle and instituted its services was a sneak preview of the things of Christ that were later revealed. These dark but glorious views of Christ were the life of the Old Testament church.

CHRIST THE GLORIOUS LOVER

Marriage has always represented the spiritual intimacy of God with his people in love and kindness.

> As a young man marries a maiden,
>   so will your sons marry you;
> as a bridegroom rejoices over his bride,
>   so will your God rejoice over you.
>   (Isaiah 62:5)[4]

The entire book of the Song of Songs is a glorious display of the love of bride and groom, and the church has always delighted to see in it an imaginative allegory or analogy of the tenderness of God with his people, and the tenacious love of his people for their God. In the New Testament Christ reveals that he is that Groom (John 3:29; Revelation 21:9), and Paul explains that marriage is a mystical picture of Christ and his bride:

> "For this reason a man will leave his father and mother and be united to his wife, and the two will become one flesh." This is a profound mystery—but *I am talking about Christ and the church.* (Ephesians 5:31–32)

Many who have drawn close to Christ see their intimacy with him described in the passion of the Song of Songs. Again, our twentieth-century[5] disdain for metaphor, imagery, and typology may make us overcautious in reading ourselves and Christ into this love song. But centuries of faithful saints who have gone before us felt no such inhibitions. Even our sober-minded Puritan fathers and mothers, who are such a faithful corrective to so many other excesses of the church in our day, let fly with mystical abandon as they relished the glory of Christ our Groom in the Song of Songs.[6]

This joyous interpretation of the Song of Songs didn't die with the Puritans. Consider "Jesus Christ the Apple Tree," a traditional American Christmas song that is a reflection on the Bridegroom based on Song of Songs 2:3. This song shows us a way to dig into the implications of a single image of Christ, and to unfold from it layer after layer of his glory.

Jesus Christ the Apple Tree

> The tree of life my soul hath seen,
> Laden with fruit, and always green:
> The trees of nature fruitless be
> Compared with Christ the apple tree.
>
> His beauty doth all things excel:
> By faith I know, but ne'er can tell
> The glory which I now can see
> In Jesus Christ the apple tree.
>
> For happiness I long have sought,
> And pleasure dearly I have bought:
> I missed of all; but now I see
> 'Tis found in Christ the apple tree.
>
> I'm weary with my former toil,
> Here I will sit and rest awhile:
> Under the shadow I will be,
> Of Jesus Christ the apple tree.
>
> This fruit doth make my soul to thrive,
> It keeps my dying faith alive;
> Which makes my soul in haste to be
> With Jesus Christ the apple tree.[7]

With shadows and images of the glory of the Lamb in the tabernacle and temple, and the Song of Songs to represent his beauty and grace and love, we have an idea of the depth of Christ's glory into which the saints of the Old Testament could see. We have no need to pity them, when we see these holy choruses of delight and admiration, these raptures of joy, this ardent affection. God provided them ways to commune with him, ways for those who believed to discover the glory of Christ. A few days, a few hours spent reflecting in them, is a wonder that excels all the treasures of the earth.

CHRIST THE GLORIOUS ANGEL OF THE LORD

Christ appeared several times to leaders of the church in the Old Testament. This was a prelude to his incarnation, but he appeared in the shape of a man to show what he would be. He didn't create a human nature and unite it to himself as a kind of "temporary incarnation"; by his divine power he took the form of a man (made of who knows what) and immediately dissolved it when he finished with it. In this way he appeared to Abraham, to Jacob, to Moses, to Joshua, and to others.[8]

And because Christ was the divine person who lived in and with the church from the beginning to the end of the Old Testament, he often demonstrated human affections to hint that a time would come when he would take on human nature. Indeed, we might almost say that after the fall nothing is said about God in the Old Testament except what relates to the future incarnation of Christ. It would have been absurd to represent God so often as a man grieving, repenting, being angry or pleased, if he never intended to take on the only nature capable of such passions.

CHRIST THE GLORIOUS VISION

The prophets saw the glory of Christ in visions. John says that Isaiah "saw Jesus' glory and spoke about him" (John 12:41), referring to the spectacular vision of Christ's glory filling and spilling out of the temple in Isaiah 6:1–5. He saw the fullness of God overflowing the body of the man Christ (compare Colossians 2:9), the temple he would destroy and rebuild in three days (John 2:19–21). When he saw this, Isaiah was overcome by dread. He was only revived by the ministry of that glorious One, when his sin was burned from him with a coal from the altar—all of this symbolic of the sacrifice and atonement of the Lamb to come (Isaiah 6:6–7). This was (and is) food for the souls of believers.

CHRIST THE GLORIOUS PROMISE

Countless promises in the Old Testament expounded the coming incarnation of Christ and his glory that we're interested in.

> For to us a child is born,
>> to us a son is given,
>> and the government will be on his shoulders.
> And he will be called
>> Wonderful Counselor, Mighty God,
>> Everlasting Father, Prince of Peace.
> Of the increase of his government and peace
>> there will be no end.
> He will reign on David's throne
>> and over his kingdom,
> establishing and upholding it

with justice and righteousness
    from that time on and forever.
The zeal of the LORD Almighty
    will accomplish this.
            (Isaiah 9:6–7)

When these promises were given, they weren't as clear as they are now; but we can see how they were fulfilled, and we have the apostles and Christ to explain them to us. Christ exactly answered all the promises of when and where he would be born, what kind of man he would be, how he would suffer and die and rise from the dead. All this is so clear that only the blindness of unbelief and pride can keep anyone from seeing Christ's glory in them.

CHRIST THE GLORIOUS LILY, LAMB, AND LION

The Old Testament is stuffed with metaphors to show the glory of Christ. Our Lord is called a Lily to show his gracious beauty in comparison to others (Song of Songs 2:1–2). He is called a Rose for the sweet savor of his love, grace, and obedience (Song of Songs 2:1). He is a Lamb who is meek and gentle, fit to be a sacrifice (Genesis 22:8); and he is a powerful Lion (Isaiah 31:4).

Poets use metaphors because they not only tell, but *show and tell.* That is, they make a stronger impression on the mind than abstract descriptions. For example, "The LORD is my Shepherd" engraves in my mind something deep that is hard to equal with an essay on God as provider and protector. Metaphors appeal to more of our senses and compel us to work at understanding them—even to *play* at uncovering their richness. So it makes sense that God in his wisdom represents powerful spiritual truth to us in natural images from the world around us. And rolling a metaphor around in your mind can be a delicious way to taste and relish the glory of Christ.

CHRIST THE GLORIOUS CENTER

By now you get the idea that I believe that Christ was the center of the Old Testament. All the promises, prophecies, and predictions about who he would be, when he would come, what he would do—along with the wisdom, grace, and love of God to the church in him—are the lifeline that runs through all the Old Testament. These were the sorts of things he opened to his disciples out of Moses and all the Prophets (Luke 24). These were the things he appealed to against his enemies: "You diligently study the Scriptures because you think that by them you possess eternal life. *These are the Scriptures that testify about me*" (John 5:39). If we can't find him in their pages, it's because a veil covers our minds. And we can't read, study, or meditate on the Old Testament to any advantage unless we try to find and behold the glory of Christ in them. Without Christ, the Old Testament is a sealed book.

This chapter is but a thimble from the ocean of the glory of the Christ in the pages of the Old Testament. Remember how Christ showed the disciples that he was the theme from Moses through the Prophets, and take these brief hints from this chapter into your own reflections. Let the glory of Christ blaze from the dusty old pages of Leviticus and Chronicles, Numbers and Lamentations, until you join with

Moses and David and Ruth and Daniel in songs of glory to the Lamb.

FOR REFLECTION AND DISCUSSION

1. Christ is the Bridegroom of the church, his beautiful bride. As his bride, answer the question posed of the beloved in Song of Songs 5:9: "How is your beloved better than others, most beautiful of women?"

2. Choose a metaphor from the Old Testament that refers to Christ. You may choose one of those mentioned in this chapter, or one of the following:

   Branch from Jesse (Isaiah 11:1)
   Everlasting Father (Isaiah 9:6)
   Prince of Peace (Isaiah 9:6)
   The Fountain (Zechariah 13:1)
   The Servant (Isaiah 52:13–15)
   The Sure Foundation (Isaiah 28:16)

   Spend time reflecting on that metaphor, and how it exposes the glory of Christ. Then write a five- or six-sentence prayer of praise to Christ that flows from the metaphor you chose.

3. Use the song "Jesus Christ the Apple Tree" (from this chapter) as a guide to your reflection on Christ. What are some aspects of his glory that are pictured here?

4. Choose one of the pieces of the furniture of the tabernacle other than the lampstand or the bread of the presence, and write four or five sentences about how it might have represented something of the glory of the Messiah to believers in the days of Moses. (Refer to Exodus 25–30.)

[9]

By Just Exchange

My true love hath my heart and I have his,
By just exchange one for the other giv'n;
I hold his dear, and mine he cannot miss,
There never was a better bargain driv'n.
—Sir Philip Sidney

AN UNJUST EXCHANGE

Jean Valjean, the hero of *Les Miserables,* is a former con-
vict running from his miserable past and from the un-
daunted Inspector Javert. He is offered an extraordinary
chance to escape both his past and Javert forever when another convicted criminal, Champmathieu, is mistakenly
identified as Jean Valjean and put on trial. Three prisoners
swear in court that Champmathieu is Jean Valjean, so it's
certain he'll be falsely convicted and punished.

Jean Valjean is tempted to let the man suffer for him. After all, he reasons, Champmathieu is clearly a criminal and deserves to be punished anyway. Jean Valjean could be free from the hot pursuit of Javert—free to do the good he now desires, such as care for the forsaken Fantine and her daughter Cosette, and to continue to help his city prosper—good things that would go undone if he walked into the courtroom and cleared Champmathieu and surrendered to the law.

But the thought of another man suffering in his place is too much for him—Jean Valjean is overwhelmed by the injustice of it and realizes that by letting even this wretch take his punishment,

> he was becoming a robber once more, and the most odious of robbers! he was robbing another man of his existence, his livelihood, his peace, and his place in the sunshine. He was becoming an assassin, he was killing, morally killing, a wretched man; he was inflicting on him the frightful living death, the open-air death, which is called the galleys.[1]

In spite of all he stood to gain, Jean Valjean could not let Champmathieu suffer in his place.

The injustice of a person suffering for someone else's crimes makes our consciences burn. Yet if you grew up in the church, I suspect that the first thing you learned in the gospel is that *"Christ died for our sins"* (1 Corinthians 15:3). And I hope that at some point in your life the phrase "Christ died for me" became precious to you. But if that is your story, then I also suspect that the phrase "Christ died for our sins" has never struck you as anything odd.

Yet think about it. *We* did something terribly wrong, and *someone else* suffered for it. Does that bother you? Suppose you and your brother are playing with your Hot Wheels™, and your Cobra Mustang beats his Viper down the track. Just as Dad walks into the room your brother calls you a slime wad. Then Dad takes off his belt and lays a solid whack of correction on *you*.

Do you sense a bit of injustice in this?

When we put it that way it sounds wrong. Yet our eternal hopes are hung on the fact that someone else paid with his life for the horrid things we did. If this truly is an injustice, what does that say about God's character? How can he be the Judge of the world if he is so cavalier in handing out punishment?

The Scriptures answer all objections and vindicate God's justice and righteousness. It wasn't just "okay" for Christ to suffer for the sins of his people, but it was right and good and just. The Scriptures teach that there's a union between Christ and his people—a union so intimate that God considers everything that Christ did and suffered as if we did and suffered it. That is, God is right to let us off the hook for our sins as if we had already paid in full the penalty for them, and to shower us with rewards as if we perfectly obeyed his law. Understanding this just exchange is a way to strengthen our faith and see the glory of Christ.

Peter tells us that "[Christ] himself bore our sins in his

body on the tree" (1 Peter 2:24) and that "Christ died for sins once for all, the righteous for the unrighteous, to bring you to God" (1 Peter 3:18). Our sense of justice balks at the thought of a good man dying for an evil man. And the Bible clearly lays the "blame" for this at God's feet: ". . . *the LORD* has laid on him the iniquity of us all" (Isaiah 53:6). How can we vindicate the justice of God in this?

To understand this problem and how God solved it, we need some background. First, all of God's chosen people, as members of humanity, came under the curse of God when Adam sinned (Romans 5:12 and following). This curse meant death, including the eternal death of hell—and no one could survive that eternal curse and be saved. It was impossible for God to simply sweep our sins under the rug. He would have had to deny his own righteousness, holiness, and truth. As Moses put it, "he does not leave the guilty unpunished" (Exodus 34:7). So in order to save his people who were justly under his curse and at the same time remain just and holy, God had to find someone else who could bear the weight of the curse for them.

This idea of a substitute taking the punishment for God's people is the cornerstone truth of the gospel, taught from Genesis through Revelation. God hinted at it in the first gospel promise of Genesis 3:15—that the Messiah would suffer (the serpent would "strike his heel")—and later spelled it out through the sacrifices and ceremonies of worship given through Moses. This is the most important thing that God's people were to learn from the sacrifices—that their guilt would have to be transferred to another in order for them to escape the punishment they deserved.[2]

BY JUST EXCHANGE

God can do nothing but what is right (Genesis 18:25). We can know what's right by watching what he does. This God who only does right has often punished some people for the sins of others. Therefore it is just, at least in some cases. In fact, God makes it plain in the Ten Commandments that he does this:

> . . . I, the LORD your God, am a jealous God, punishing the children for the sin of the fathers to the third and fourth generation of those who hate me. . . . (Exodus 20:5)

Jeremiah affirmed that this happened:

> Our fathers sinned and are no more,
> and we bear their punishment.
> (Lamentations 5:7)

And there are enough other examples to show that these cases aren't exceptions. When God sent Judah into captivity in Babylon, he punished them for the sins of their forefathers, particularly the sins committed in the days of Manasseh (2 Kings 23:26–27). God cursed Canaan for the sin of his father Ham (Genesis 9:25). Saul's seven sons were put to death for their father's bloody cruelty (2 Samuel 21:9, 14). God sent an angel to destroy seventy thousand people for the king's sin, although David said, "I am the one who has sinned and done wrong. These are but sheep. What have they done? Let your hand fall upon me and my family" (2 Samuel

24:15–17). In spite of the legendary wickedness of Ahab, God said of him, "Have you noticed how Ahab has humbled himself before me? Because he has humbled himself, I will not bring this disaster in his day, but I will bring it on his house in the days of his son" (1 Kings 21:29). It was the same for the children and infants who were destroyed in the flood, or in the fires of Sodom and Gomorrah. And Jesus said that when God cut off the nation of Israel, he punished that final generation for all the bloody persecutions from the beginning of the world.

> Therefore this generation will be held responsible for the blood of all the prophets that has been shed since the beginning of the world, from the blood of Abel to the blood of Zechariah, who was killed between the altar and the sanctuary. Yes, I tell you, this generation will be held responsible for it all. (Luke 11:50–51)

Each of these demonstrates God's terrifying justice. They prove beyond doubt that our righteous, true, and holy God will sometimes punish some people for the sins of others. Therefore, it can't be wrong.

WHEN IS THIS EXCHANGE JUST?

So it isn't always wrong to punish someone for the sins of others—but neither is it always right. There has to be a special reason, a peculiar connection or union between those who sin and those who are punished. This union must include an *intimate relationship* and a *close mutual interest.*

The intimate relationship must be as close as that between parents and children, as in most of the examples in the Scriptures, or between a king and his subjects, as in the case of David. In these cases the sinners and the sufferers are treated as one body, so that the backside answers for what the hand steals. And those who sin must have a close mutual interest with those who are punished for their sins—so close that they feel the punishment themselves, as a father would be tormented to see his son beaten. Think of the burden you would feel in your soul if God said to you, as he said to his grumbling people in the wilderness,

> Your children will be shepherds here for forty years, suffering for your unfaithfulness, until the last of your bodies lies in the desert. (Numbers 14:33)

Wouldn't you grieve at the thought of what your sins brought on your children? That would be the sting of your own punishment.

The union between Christ and the church is more intimate and has more mutual interest than any relationship between people in the history of the world. Because of this, it was just and right for God to slay his Lamb for our sins and to count his suffering and death as our very own.

We can distinguish three ways that people can be joined: by a natural union, by a spiritual or mystical union, or by an agreed union (as in the case of a covenant). Christ is singularly united to us in all three.

1. The first union is natural. God made all people "from one man" (Acts 17:26) so that there's an alliance among us all. Every other person is our brother or neighbor and is due our kindness (Luke 10:36). By his incarnation, Christ shared this natural union with the church:

> Since the children have flesh and blood, he too shared in their humanity so that by his death he might destroy him who holds the power of death—that is, the devil—and free those who all their lives were held in slavery by their fear of death. (Hebrews 2:14–15)

So "both the one who makes men holy and those who are made holy are of the same family" (Hebrews 2:11). It was our Lord's unmeasured humility, as we have already seen, to take part in our nature with us. And although his union with us in our humanity is "natural," there are two things that distinguish our union with him from our natural union with all humankind.

First, this natural union between Christ and the church didn't come about by nature, but by a voluntary act of his will. Our union with others is necessary. We are all brothers and sisters, whether or not we want to be, because we are human beings. It's a fact of life and has nothing to do with choice. With the Lord Christ it was different (see Hebrews 2:11, 14–15). So that he might rescue us from death, he freely chose to take on our flesh and blood and a natural union with us. Therefore, although you might think it wrong for one person to suffer for others simply because they are also people and they are forced to share this nature, things are different with Christ. He is united to the church by his own free choice.

Second, Christ took on our flesh in order to obey and suffer in the place of the church. Hebrews 2:14–15 says he took our flesh *"so that* by his death he might destroy him who holds the power of death . . . and free those who all their lives were held in slavery by their fear of death." This was the only reason for his natural union with the church; and this makes his union with us incomparably closer than any union between others.

2. The second union is spiritual. This union is analogous to the most real or moral unions between other persons or things. What I mean by a "real" union is like that between the head of a body and its hands, or the trunk of a tree and its branches. A "moral" union is like that between a husband and wife (which is both moral and real). The Scriptures teach that such a union between Christ and his church is the foundation of his suffering in our place. In Ephesians 5 Paul calls the church Christ's bride and says that he "gave himself up for her" (verse 25). Since he was the head and husband of the church, the only way he could sanctify and save her was by his blood and sufferings—and it was righteous that what he did and suffered should be considered ours.

3. The third union is contractual or covenantal. People can be joined by legal documents such as a power of attorney or a contract with an agent, which allow them to designate someone else to act on their behalf. Christ was united to us by a bond like this that the Father made with him:

> Others became priests without any oath, but he became a priest with an oath when God said to him:

> "The Lord has sworn
>   and will not change his mind:
> 'You are a priest forever.' "
>
> Because of this oath, Jesus has become the guarantee of a better covenant. (Hebrews 7:20–22)

In this covenantal bond, sealed by God's oath, Christ took it on himself to suffer for us, in our place, on our behalf—to give to God whatever God required from us—in order to save and sanctify us. Because of this contract it was perfectly just for him to be punished for our sins.

This is the holy mystery of transferring the guilt and punishment of the sins of the church to One who was in every way innocent, pure, and righteous. This just exchange is the life, soul, and center of the gospel. In this exchange Christ is immeasurably glorious and precious to us who believe. No heart can conceive, no tongue can express, the glory of Christ in this.

THERE NEVER WAS A BETTER BARGAIN DRIV'N

I've already spoken of the Lamb's infinite humility and love in obeying and suffering for us,[3] so let's move on to consider the greatness of this union in some of its fruit.

1. This union exalts the righteousness of God in the forgiveness of sins. Some of our highest thoughts of God are of his justice in rule and government. It is God's right to punish sin as it deserves, and punishing sin was one of the first things he did in governing his creation. He expelled Adam and Eve from Paradise (Genesis 3)—but even before that he had already punished Satan and the angels who rebelled with him.

Because of the fall, all God's elect are sinners; we all sinned in Adam as he represented us, and we continue to sin ourselves. What should the God of justice do to us? Should he wink at our crimes and rebellion and leave us all unpunished? If so, how would that square with his justice, which didn't spare Adam in the beginning or even one angel who sinned? The righteousness of God on the one hand and the forgiveness of sin on the other seem so contradictory that many stumble over it (see Romans 10:3–4). How can we reconcile the truth that God "does not leave the guilty unpunished" (Exodus 34:7) with the statement that God "justifies the wicked" (Romans 4:5)?

But when Christ unites himself to the church and takes on her punishment, we see a glorious harmony between God's righteousness and his forgiveness. Because of this union it was perfectly just that "the LORD . . . laid on him the iniquity of us all" (Isaiah 53:6), and that he freely and graciously pardoned us. In the slaughter of the Lamb for us we see the highest magnification of the honor of both God's justice and his mercy. Not a single sin is left unpunished[4]— yet we revel in his redeeming grace.

> But now a righteousness from God, apart from law, has been made known, to which the Law and the Prophets testify. This righteousness from God comes through faith in Jesus Christ to all who believe.

There is no difference, for all have sinned and fall short of the glory of God, and are justified freely by his grace through the redemption that came by Christ Jesus. God presented him as a sacrifice of atonement, through faith in his blood. He did this to demonstrate his justice, because in his forbearance he had left the sins committed beforehand unpunished—he did it to demonstrate his justice at the present time, so as to be just and the one who justifies those who have faith in Jesus. (Romans 3:21–26)

In solving this problem Christ is glorious in the sight of God, angels, and human beings. In him there is at the same time, in the same divine act, a bubbling over of justice and mercy. The apparent inconsistency between the righteousness of God and the salvation of sinners, which troubles the consciences of some to the point that they reject Christ and are eternally lost, is removed and taken away. In his cross, divine holiness and vindictive justice are demonstrated against the Lamb of God; and out of his triumph gush grace and mercy. This glory ravishes the hearts and satisfies the souls of believers. For what more can we want, what more perfectly calms and steadies our souls, than to see in one view God eternally pleased in the declaration of his righteousness and the exercise of his mercy?

In due apprehensions hereof let my soul live—in the faith hereof let me die, and let present admiration of this glory make way for the eternal enjoyment of it in its beauty and fulness.[5]

2. This union is glorious because in it we see the perfection of God's law. When we fell in Adam, we were no longer able to keep the law that God required of us.[6] If his law had been left broken and unfulfilled, no one could ever see the wisdom, holiness, and righteousness of God in giving it. What could be less becoming a perfect God than to give a law that never was to be fulfilled by those to whom he gave it? How would it show his wisdom if he promised eternal rewards for keeping his law, but none could ever keep it? We could never keep it; but through the obedience of Christ, because of his union with us, the law was fulfilled in us by being fulfilled for us—to the glory of God.

> For what the law was powerless to do in that it was weakened by the sinful nature, God did by sending his own Son in the likeness of sinful man to be a sin offering. And so he condemned sin in sinful man, in order that the righteous requirements of the law might be fully met in us, who do not live according to the sinful nature but according to the Spirit. (Romans 8:3–4)

A view of Christ keeping the law for us is our glorious anchor. When our souls are beaten down with fear and our consciences troubled by temptation and sin, our faith can cling to Christ's obedience. He satisfied every demand of God. Because he is joined to us in this intimate union and obeyed for us, we have nothing to fear from the most terrifying threats of the law. Through our union with him we have peace that passes understanding.

By just exchange one for the other giv'n . . .
There never was a better bargain driv'n.

FOR REFLECTION AND DISCUSSION

1. Christ is the Bridegroom of the church, his beautiful bride. As his bride, answer the question posed of the beloved in Song of Songs 5:9: "How is your beloved better than others, most beautiful of women?"

2. How would you answer an unbeliever (or a troubled believer) who objected to the gospel on the grounds that it was not just for someone to pay for someone else's crime?

3. What is it that makes Christ's *natural* union with us closer than the union we share with any other human being?

4. What is it that makes Christ's *spiritual* union with us closer than the union we share with any other human being?

5. What is it that makes Christ's *contractual* union with us closer than the union we share with any other human being?

6. What does the oath in Hebrews 7:20–22 mean to your faith?

7. How does Christ solve the apparent conflict between God's mercy and his justice?

Charitas Nimia: *or the Dear Bargain*

Lord, what is man? why should he cost thee
    So dear? what had his ruin lost thee?
Lord, what is man, that thou hast over-bought
      So much a thing of naught?

    Love is too kind, I see, and can
Make but a simple merchantman;
'Twas for such sorry merchandise
Bold painters have put out his eyes.
Alas, sweet Lord, what were't to thee,
If there were no such worms as we?
Heaven ne'ertheless still heaven would be,
    Should mankind dwell
    In the deep hell,
What have his woes to do with thee?

    Let him go weep
    O'er his own wounds;
    Seraphims will not sleep
Nor spheres let fall their faithful rounds.

    Still would the youthful spirits sing,
And still thy spacious palace ring:
Still would those beauteous ministers of light
    Burn all as bright,

    And bow their flaming heads before thee;
Still Thrones and Dominations would adore thee;

Still would those ever-wakeful sons of fire
    Keep warm thy praise
    Both nights and days,
And teach thy loved name to their noble lyre.

    Let froward dust then do its kind,
And give itself for sport to the proud wind.
Why should a piece of peevish care plead shares
In the Eternity of thy old cares?
Why shouldst thou bow thy awful breast to see
What mine own madnesses have done with me?

    Should not the King still keep his throne
Because some desperate fool's undone?
Or will the world's illustrious eyes
Weep for every worm that dies?

    Will the gallant sun
    E'er the less glorious run?
Will he hang down his golden head
Or e'er the sooner seek his western bed,
    Because some foolish fly
    Grows wanton and will die?

    If I were lost in misery,
What was it to thy heaven and thee?
What was it to thy precious blood
If my foul heart called for a flood?

What if my faithless soul and I
    Would needs fall in

With guilt and sin?
What did the Lamb that he should die?
What did the Lamb that he should need,
When the Wolf sins, himself to bleed?

If my base lust
Bargained with death and well be-seeming dust,
Why should the white
Lamb's bosom write
The purple name
Of my sin's shame?

Why should the unstained breast make good
My blushes with his own heart-blood?

O, my Saviour, make me see
How dearly thou hast paid for me,

That lost again my life may prove
As then in death, so now in love.

(Richard Crashaw)

[1 O]

The Glory of Glories

All the king's horses, and all the king's men,
Couldn't put Humpty together again.
—Mother Goose

It's hard enough to mend a broken egg.[1] But what if, as
Bob Dylan said, "Everything's Broken"?

> Broken hands
> On broken ploughs,
> Broken treaties,
> Broken vows,
> Broken pipes,
> Broken tools,
> People bendin'

Broken rules.
Hound dog howlin',
Bullfrog croakin'—
Everything is broken.[2]

What if instead of Humpty-Dumpty it was all the king's men who fell—could anyone put them back together again? I'm not talking about sewing arms and legs back onto torsos, a miracle of modern science. I'm talking about restoring the big fall—when we tumbled with Adam away from God and his holy angels. I'm talking about making right everything that's wrong with the world, from Hitler and Stalin to children born with no brains to AIDS to global warming.

I'm sure by now you know just the Man for the job. Paul told the Ephesians that God, with all wisdom and understanding, has

> made known to us the mystery of his will according to his good pleasure, which he purposed in Christ, to be put into effect when the times will have reached their fulfillment—*to bring all things in heaven and on earth together under one head, even Christ.* (Ephesians 1:9–10)

Philosophers, scientists, psychologists, and politicians are all trying to patch things up. By God's grace they succeed now and then at restoring peace between two nations, or wiping out smallpox, or helping troubled people to cope with day-to-day life, and we rightly thank God for these gifts. But it is the glory of Christ that he'll one day make everything whole again—and make it even better than it was in the beginning.

So that we can get a better look at his glory in this, let's review the history of the world.

A TALE OF TWO FAMILIES

Try to imagine what it was like before God created the heavens and the earth.

Is your head aching yet? If not, you aren't trying. It's not easy to think away the universe. But if you could, what would be left? Nothing. Nothing but God, that is. Before he created anything, God was. Father, Son, and Holy Spirit existed from eternity, one God in three persons in glorious perfection of love and harmony and being. And God held within himself all being, power, goodness, wisdom—all the perfection that we now adore in him.

When God made the heavens and the earth, he gave the universe being and goodness by his power and wisdom—and he did this in order to show his glory. This was the first time God gave of himself to anything outside himself, and it was glorious.

> The heavens declare the glory of God;
>> the skies proclaim the work of his hands.
>>> (Psalm 19:1)

> For since the creation of the world God's invisible qualities—his eternal power and divine nature—have been clearly seen, being understood from what has been made. . . . (Romans 1:20)

Now this creation of God's was a curious living system, with all its interlocking pieces depending on each other for their energy and sustenance. These are the ecosystems and symbiotic relationships and food chains and solar systems that we studied in eighth-grade biology. But what they didn't teach us in secular science books is that all of these interdependent systems depend on God himself as the eternal fountain of being, power, and goodness. God is no less glorious in keeping the universe working from moment to moment than he is in creating it all. Take away God's sustaining hand and the universe disappears without a trace—faster than the lights go out when you hit the switch.

> He has shown kindness by giving you rain from heaven and crops in their seasons; he provides you with plenty of food and fills your hearts with joy. (Acts 14:17)

> The God who made the world and everything in it is the Lord of heaven and earth and does not live in temples built by hands. And he is not served by human hands, as if he needed anything, because *he himself gives all men life and breath and everything else.* . . . "For *in him we live and move and have our being.*" As some of your own poets have said, "We are his offspring." (Acts 17:24–28)

> The Son is the radiance of God's glory and the exact representation of his being, *sustaining all things by his powerful word.* (Hebrews 1:3)

When God gave existence from his perfect being, wisdom, and power to this tangible, visible creation, he did it to show us his glory. He created us with minds that could learn from the creation around us and the acts of providence in creation that he exists and is powerful, righteous, just, good, and merciful (Romans 1:20). God intended for us to see his glory in the world.

God created two families of beings with minds that could know him and give him glory. And he made two homes, heaven and earth, each suited to one of these families of beings. He placed his angels in heaven and humankind on the earth. God gave humankind authority to rule over everything on earth, as a constant declaration of the image and glory of God to all creation. Angels had a similar role in heaven, and it was their way to glorify God.

This creation was, in God's own judgment, "very good" (Genesis 1:31). And one beauty of this original setup was that there was nothing between God and his angels and human beings. There was no need for a mediator (see Genesis 3:8).

This beautiful order, this union between the two families of God, was shattered by sin. Many angels and all humankind rejected their dependence on God and rebelled against him. Because God was no longer the center of their lives, they began to devour each other in hatred (see the story of Cain and Abel in Genesis 4, and the rest of history). God cursed the earth and everything in it. The angels who remained obedient to God remained in heaven with him, but all men and women were shut out of God's glorious presence. God even put an angel at the entrance of the Garden of Eden to keep them out (Genesis 3:24).

God showed his terrible severity by righteously rejecting the fallen angels forever, but he showed mercy by determining to recover some of humankind. But as God rescued some men and women, he left them separated from the angels—one family in heaven, another family on earth. But his plan was to bring them together under a single head, so that these two families of wonderful creatures would make one glorious family. This is what Paul was talking about in Ephesians 1:9–10 (quoted above), and again in Colossians 1:19–20: "God was pleased . . . through him to reconcile to himself all things, whether things on earth or things in heaven. . . ."

This new head of everything in heaven and earth is Jesus Christ, the Son of God made man (see 1 Corinthians 11:3; Ephesians 1:22–23). This glory was reserved for him; no one else was worthy of it.

> He is before all things, and in him all things hold together. And he is the head of the body, the church; he is the beginning and the firstborn from among the dead, so that in everything he might have the supremacy. For God was pleased to have all his fullness dwell in him. . . . (Colossians 1:17–19)

As head of God's restored family, Christ was given all power in heaven and earth, and the perfection of grace and glory. We (and the angels) get nothing from God—no commands, no power, no grace, no goodness—except what comes through Christ. In him we live, on him we depend, to him we bow.[3] Of course, angels and human beings are different, so Christ became head of each in different ways. The angels who didn't fall into sin didn't need a redeemer as we did. And since all of us had shared in Adam's sin and fall, we couldn't be kept in glory by Christ as the angels were. But in each case Christ is the head and brings everything together.

This is more than putting the egg back together again. In Christ everything broken will be repaired.

THE GLORY OF GLORIES

Our abridged history of the world barely touches the mysterious work of God's wisdom in restoring everything in Jesus Christ. But it's enough to see that Christ's glory in this is light-years above our highest thoughts. Still, by faith we can reflect on his glory, meager as our meditations might be. Consider his glory.

Christ alone could bear the weight of this glory. No mere creature in heaven or earth was fit to be head of the whole new creation. No one else could stand in the place of God, have all things depend on him, and have all things submit to him in such a way that nothing comes from God to his creatures except through him. So when the Spirit speaks of Christ's glory, he describes him in terms that make it clear that there's no one like him:

> The Son is the radiance of God's glory and the exact representation of his being, sustaining all things by his powerful word. (Hebrews 1:3)

> He is the image of the invisible God, the firstborn over all creation. For by him all things were created:

things in heaven and on earth, visible and invisible, whether thrones or powers or rulers or authorities; all things were created by him and for him. He is before all things, and in him all things hold together. (Colossians 1:15–17)

Christ's glory in this is his greatest glory of all. God planned for his eternal Son to become man. We know that he did this in order to rescue his church from sin. But now we see that there's more to God's plan: He's not simply going to redeem his people, which is wondrous enough; he's going to bring everything together in him—the whole creation. He is the fountain of everything and holds everything together forever! How can I capture in words the divine beauty, order, and harmony of this? Communion between angels and human beings; the shower of life, grace, power, mercy, and consolation to the church; the rule of everything for the glory of God—all depend on Christ restoring everything. This is the glory God designed for his Son in the incarnation, and no glory can compare to it.

Since this is his highest glory, reflecting on it should move us with delight and joy. To see him in the place of God as the supreme head of the whole creation, ruling and caring for it, should refresh every believer's soul.

In this Christ restores the glory of God in creation that was violated by sin. Have you gasped in awe of a sunrise draped over the Sangre de Cristo Mountains? Have you been stopped in your tracks by a forest of towering redwoods? Have your eyes grown moist with joy at the birth of your first child? It's unthinkable, but these are just the shadows of the glory of the original creation. Everything around us and in us is groaning under the curse of sin (Romans 8:20–22). The beauty of the first creation shouted the being, goodness, wisdom, and eternal power of God. This was all vandalized by sin, more unthinkably crass than someone taking a machete to the *Mona Lisa.*

But when Christ restores everything, he'll make the heavens and the earth even more glorious than they were in the beginning! This is the glory of Christ.

Christ is the only way we know God's infinite wisdom. The wisdom of God is always and in everything infinite. God doesn't (and he can't) do one thing more wisely than he does another. He wasn't wiser in creating humankind than he was in making algae. In the first creation, this unlimited wisdom was united to his unlimited power: "How many are your works, O Lord! In wisdom you made them *all"* (Psalm 104:24). But when the beauty and glory of the first creation were defaced, it took greater treasures of wisdom to repair the damage. So in putting everything back together in Christ and pouring on it more glory than ever, God is doing the highest thing he'll ever do with his creatures. Paul explains that this is the only way we can know the fullness of God's wisdom:

> This grace was given me: to preach to the Gentiles
> the unsearchable riches of Christ, and to make plain
> to everyone the administration of this mystery,
> which for ages past was kept hidden in God, who

created all things. His intent was that now, through the church, *the manifold wisdom of God should be made known* to the rulers and authorities in the heavenly realms, according to his eternal purpose which he accomplished in Christ Jesus our Lord. (Ephesians 3:8–11)

This is even the way the angels know the fullness of God's wisdom—they couldn't have known it before sin came into the world, because there was nothing to repair. They didn't know there was something beyond the original glory of creation. But in Christ, in this plan to restore all creation, is "hidden all the treasures of wisdom and knowledge" (Colossians 2:3). Jesus is glorious in this, and will be through eternity.

Christ will keep the new creation in glory forever. As wonderful as the first creation was, it was capable of being ruined. The sin of angels and human beings scarred and twisted its beauty. But now everything that belongs to this new creation, every believer in the world and every angel in heaven, are secured from ruin. Christ will glorify us and keep us glorified forever.

MORE THAN I CAN EVER SAY

Who can talk about these things with the words they deserve? Who can describe the glory of Christ? I have no more chapters to write of Christ's glory, although I've hardly begun. My hope now is that you and I will reflect on his glory through the looking glass of the Scriptures, see it with the eyes of our faith, and see it at least clearly enough that we'll admire and adore him every day of our lives.

For Reflection and Discussion

1. Christ is the Bridegroom of the church, his beautiful bride. As his bride, answer the question posed of the beloved in Song of Songs 5:9: "How is your beloved better than others, most beautiful of women?"

2. What about the glory of Christ in restoring everything makes this glory greater than all others?

3. How is it that Christ's glory in bringing together angels and human beings in one body shows God's manifold wisdom?

We've by no means come to

the end of the glory of Christ,

but it's time to think about what's

at the end of the road. What we can

see of Christ now by faith, glorious

as it is, can't begin to compare

with what we'll see in heaven.

[11]

To Live Divided, with but Half a Heart

. . . to live
Divided, with but half a heart,
Till we shall meet and never part.
—Henry King

Exiled to the Eastern Front

Olomouc lies in the center of Moravia, three hours east of Prague by train, twenty-four hours by planes, trains, and automobiles from my bride in New Mexico. During my two-month sabbatical there one winter, my wife and I exchanged some love letters that nearly melted the snow around my flat. Her letters to me were my food and drink, the sunshine that broke through the frozen gray sky to light my day. Every day at noon I charged up the five flights of stairs to find the housekeeper to ask for my mail. When I saw my name formed in my wife's hand on an envelope, I went straight to my apartment and devoured every word and line, feasting on our love.

As delicious as her letters were, they weren't enough. Within the first week of my sabbatical, I began to punctuate my journal entries with groans and sighs of missing her. Those groans and sighs grew until the final days, when I wrote, "All I want is to grab her and never let her go." Love letters are no match for the real thing—face to face, staring into your lover's eyes, her warm body against your own.

The "not enoughness" of love-letters is like the way we see Christ by faith in this life. We can bask for hours in his glory as the God-man, or as the only face of God to us, or as the wisdom of God, or as the love of God—and that glory feeds, comforts, and delights our souls. But it isn't enough. There's something more that we can't have in this life, and it makes us ache to be with him. Lovers of Christ like David and Paul knew the deepest experiences of his glory and love that can be known by faith, yet they cried out for more.

> My soul thirsts for God, for the living God.
> When can I go and meet with God?
> (Psalm 42:2)

> I desire to depart and be with Christ, which is better by far. . . . (Philippians 1:23)

What David and Paul felt was the frustration of living by faith and not by sight (2 Corinthians 5:7). We live before

God in this life by faith alone. By faith we take part in God's grace, holiness, and joy; but someday, by sight, we'll take hold of eternal happiness and glory.

With faith now and sight in heaven we take hold of the same thing: the glory of Christ. By faith we "see" his glory in this life, as we meditate on him as he's revealed to us in the Scriptures. That's what this book is about. But in this chapter we'll explore the difference between the glimpse of the glory of Christ we have in this world by faith and the vision we'll have of it in the next—and it's all the difference in the world.

BUT A POOR REFLECTION

Although we've spent most of this book celebrating the joy and comfort and strength we have from our view of the glory of Christ by faith in this world, the view we have is an obscure, dark image, like seeing someone reflected in the freshly polished hood of a car. Paul didn't have in mind the refined mirrors of our day when he said,

> Now we see but *a poor reflection as in a mirror;* then we shall see face to face. Now I know in part; then I shall know fully, even as I am fully known. (1 Corinthians 13:12)

Face to face is what we long for, but here we see only a reflection—and a poor reflection at that! We can certainly see Christ in the gospel—and through these chapters I hope you've seen that he is altogether lovely, the Desired of the nations, the Rose of Sharon, the Morning Star. Yet the image we can see of him by faith is only a fuzzy, fading photograph when compared to his unclouded glory in heaven.

The word that Paul uses in 1 Corinthians 13:12 to describe the quality of our view of Christ in this life is the word from which we derive our word *enigma*. An enigma is a riddle or paradoxical saying. This suggests another way to think of the difference between seeing Christ by faith and seeing him face to face: Seeing him by faith is like reading T. S. Eliot's *The Waste Land* or William Faulkner's *The Sound and the Fury* or some bicycle assembly instructions written by someone who doesn't speak English; seeing the Lamb face to face is like reading E. B. White's *Stuart Little.*

But let's be clear that it isn't the gospel that's dark and obscure—in the gospel Christ is plainly set forth crucified, exalted, glorified. Paul isn't talking about the *way* or *means* of the revelation of Christ to us, but the way we *comprehend* that revelation. We receive it by faith, and since our faith is weak and imperfect, we comprehend the glory of Christ in the gospel as people understand a paradox or a parable— imperfectly and with difficulty. God's servant Job nailed it on the head when he said, "How faint the whisper we hear of him!" (Job 26:14). We're so weak that we can only take in a bit of his glory, and even when we do take it in we can't long hold on to it. This is the frustration of walking by faith, not by sight.

Like the frustrated beloved in Solomon's Song, we catch only glimpses of Christ, as if he's standing behind a wall, or looking through a window, or peering through the lattice (Song of Songs 2:9)—our view of him is blocked or patchy or unstable. The weakness of our sinful flesh is the wall between us and our Beloved, and it has to be destroyed before we can see him face to face. But sometimes he looks through the window or the lattice of the gospel, and we get a refreshing glimpse of him. Still, it's not enough, and we cry with David,

> As the deer pants for streams of water,
>   so my soul pants for you, O God.
> My soul thirsts for God, for the living God.
>   When can I go and meet with God?
>   (Psalm 42:1–2)

FACE TO FACE, WITH NEW EYES

Things are going to change. Someday we'll look on Christ with a steady, fixed gaze. Instead of seeing a reflected image of him in the gospel, we'll see him "face to face," which Paul contrasts with the "poor [enigmatic] reflection" we see now (1 Corinthians 13:12). We'll see him as he is (1 John 3:2), not just an incomplete description of him. We won't even see just a brief glimpse of his back passing in front of us, as Moses did (Exodus 33:21–23)—we'll see him and talk with him as you might talk with your neighbor in front of your house.

And we'll see him with the eyes in our heads—it won't be some "spiritual apprehension":

> I know that my Redeemer lives,
>   and that in the end he will stand upon the earth.
> And after my skin has been destroyed,
>   yet in my flesh I will see God;

> I myself will see him
>> with my own eyes—I, and not another.
> How my heart yearns within me!
>>> (Job 19:25–27)

God will restore and glorify our eyesight in heaven until we can out-see the eagle. And he'll do this for one reason: so that we can eternally take in the Lamb and his glory, in answer to our Lord's prayer in John 17:24. With the very eyes that you now see the tokens of Christ in the bread and wine of communion, you'll one day see him in the flesh. Doesn't that give you goose bumps? And you won't just see his human nature. You'll see his divine person as it is united with his human nature. You'll see the perfection of infinite wisdom, love, and power in him. All the glories of Christ that we have so weakly and faintly reflected on in this life will fill our eyes forever.

To be face to face with Christ is what we pine for. We want, like Paul, "to depart and be with Christ, which is better by far" (Philippians 1:23). We would rather "be away from the body and at home with the Lord" (2 Corinthians 5:8), where we'll enjoy the inexpressibly longed-for sight of the Lamb in his glory. Those who don't long for it, whose souls and minds aren't often distracted by yearnings to be in heaven with Christ, whose thoughts of seeing him aren't their relief in trouble and their best joy—such people have never even seen a glimpse of him by faith.

For us to be able to see him in glory, we'll have to be changed. "Now we are children of God, and what we will be has not yet been made known" (1 John 3:2). Without this we can't see him as he is. When he was transfigured and had on his human nature some reflections of his divine glory, his disciples weren't refreshed by it but "fell facedown to the ground, terrified" (Matthew 17:6). They saw his glory, but when Peter started talking about it, "he did not know what he was saying" (Luke 9:30–33). The reason was that no one in this life has the eyes, either spiritual or physical, to see and take in the glory of Christ face to face.

In fact, if the Lord Jesus walked up beside you right now in his majesty and glory and tapped you on the shoulder, it wouldn't comfort and strengthen you. You aren't fit or ready to bear his glory face to face. His beloved apostle John had leaned against him many times in his affection as his close friend; but when Jesus appeared to him in his glory, John "fell at his feet as though dead" (Revelation 1:17). And when Jesus appeared to Paul, all that Paul could say about it was that he "saw a light from heaven, brighter than the sun," and that he and his companions fell to the ground (Acts 26:13–14). This was one reason why during his ministry here on earth Christ cloaked his glory under the weakness of the flesh and all sorts of sufferings—to spare us from seeing his glory before we were ready.

For now we're only fit to know the Son by the Spirit. We no longer know him through the physical means of the worship ceremonies of the Old Testament—we're beyond that. And we don't know him in his bodily presence as his disciples did in Galilee twenty centuries ago—we're also beyond that. We sometimes wish that we could see him in his flesh as the disciples did back then, but Jesus himself said that what we have now is better by far: "But I tell you the truth:

It is for your good that I am going away. Unless I go away, the Counselor will not come to you; but if I go, I will send him to you" (John 16:7). The view we have of his glory now by faith is better than what they had of his humanity with their eyes. Still, it isn't enough.

A NEW MIND

In order to see the Lamb in his glories, your mind will have to be overhauled. God will literally change your mind. He'll drive away the last shadow of ignorance, firm up the slightest unsteadiness, remove every obstruction that has ever hindered or blocked or blurred your sight of Christ by faith.

Our flesh makes our minds vain, dark, corrupt—unable to discern anything spiritual (1 Corinthians 2:14). When we're born again into the kingdom, the darkness of original sin that blinded us is healed so that we can see truly—but that healing isn't finished. We're like the blind man whom Jesus healed in two stages: from being blind as a bat he was able to see men walking around, but they looked like trees; Jesus touched him a second time and everything was crystal clear (Mark 8:22–25). So we can see spiritual things and discern spiritual truth and even take hold of Christ by faith—but still frustrated by error and weakness, we groan for that second healing touch. When he reaches out his hand again, he won't leave the least trace of a scar or wound (Ephesians 5:27).

Try to imagine how precious this will be. Today our minds are slow to pray. When we finally turn our thoughts to spiritual things, they can hardly stay put for two minutes; they flit about to the overdue project at work, the hateful words of a neighbor, the schemes of how to spend $23 million when the Lotto numbers come up right. But when our minds are made new, nothing will be able to divert our eyes from Christ and his glory. We won't grow tired or bored. We won't be tempted to look around for something better to do. Our thoughts will be pure gold. And just one such thought of the Lamb will fill us with more satisfaction and pleasure than all our best thoughts in this world rolled together.

A New Body

When our bodies are glorified we'll see our Redeemer with our eyes (Job 19:25–27). We don't yet know how our bodies will be changed (1 Corinthians 15:35–49), but God will make them ready to bear and enjoy eternal happiness in his presence. When Stephen was martyred he tasted some of this glory before he died. When he was brought to trial before the council, "All who were sitting in the Sanhedrin looked intently at Stephen, and they saw that his face was like the face of an angel" (Acts 6:15). He was transfigured to some degree, not unlike Jesus in Matthew 17. And by this beginning of his glorification his eyes grew so keen and powerful that he stared through the inconceivable distance between earth and heaven, and "saw the glory of God, and Jesus standing at the right hand of God" (Acts 7:55). Who, then, can say what will be the power of our sense of sight when perfectly glorified; or what sweetness and refreshment we'll take in through our renewed eyes?

If you could travel back to any time in history and any place on the planet, when and where would you go? My father and I used to play this game. He'd talk about wanting to see King Arthur in Camelot, but then always come back to Jesus—he wanted to see Jesus in the flesh. Who of us wouldn't give the world for such a trip? And when the disciples saw our Lord in his body, they saw what "many prophets and righteous men longed to see" (Matthew 13:17). As remarkable a privilege as it was, it's little when compared to what Stephen saw when he peered into heaven to see the Lord Jesus in his uncloaked glory. So how wonderful will it be, then, when our eyes are gloriously purified and strengthened beyond Stephen's!

This Present Darkness

This glorious vision is what we pant after like the deer for water (Psalm 42:1). It's the answer to the Lord's dying prayer (John 17:24), and the ultimate satisfaction for our souls. How is it different from our glorious glimpses of Christ by faith now?

Here we're loaded down with the burden of our weakness. Our remaining ignorance and frailty handicap our faith. Even in those best moments, when heaven seems to break through and we adore and admire Christ in his glory, filled with wonder at his beauty, seemingly transported to heaven by his gentle and courageous love for us—even then our worship is punctuated with our groans for deliverance:

> We ourselves, who have the firstfruits of the Spirit, groan inwardly as we wait eagerly for our adoption as sons, the redemption of our bodies. For in this hope we were saved. But hope that is seen is no hope at all. Who hopes for what he already has? (Romans 8:23–24)

As we grow in faith and spiritual understanding, we grow more aware of our burdens, and we more urgently groan for deliverance—for the perfect freedom of the sons of God. This is a mark of those who are mature in the Spirit. The nearer anyone is to heaven, the more he or she longs to be there, because Christ is there. The more frequent and steady our views of him by faith, the more we long and groan for the obliteration of every obstruction that clouds our view of him.

In fact, we can't think of Christ without being ashamed of and troubled by our own thoughts—they seem so confused, unsteady, and imperfect. We groan that we can't think better about him, can't think longer about him, aren't moved more deeply by him. Oh! when will we come to him? When will we be with him and not have to leave? When will we see him as he is? Usually this trouble and groaning follows or even fills our best meditations—a trouble that I ask God never to deliver me from before I die.

The hearts of believers moved by the glory of Christ are like a compass needle that can't fix on the pole. Their hearts can't be still, they can no longer be satisfied to be away from Jesus. Their hearts pant and sigh and groan and weep in prayers and meditations. They continually turn toward Christ, their pole, but never quite come to rest.

A Cloud of Witnesses

We've already seen in chapter 8 that Old Testament believers had precious revelations of the glory of Christ—but they were far more obscure and incomplete than what we now cherish in the finished Scriptures. Old Testament believers could see Christ, but under the cloak of shadows and types and symbols and metaphors. Still, it was the food of their faith, and they "searched intently and with the greatest care" to find what the Spirit had to say about Christ (1 Peter 1:10–11). By their example they teach us to search out the glory of Christ while we still struggle against ignorance and weakness.

They had great spiritual wisdom. They rejoiced and gloried in the ceremonies of worship. They looked on them as their highest privilege and gave their hearts to them as the designs of divine wisdom and love, and as a shadow of good things to come. But at the same time, they longed for the time of restoration to come, when they would see and enjoy the wonders symbolized in their worship. And those who didn't look forward, who rested in and trusted in the shadows themselves, were rejected by God.

Don't you admire Moses and Ruth and David and Isaiah? Think of how dark some of the Old Testament seems to you now, even though you have the gospel to explain it and the Spirit to lift the veil. How much more mysterious it must have been to them—yet they saw "the things promised . . . and welcomed them from a distance" (Hebrews 11:13). They reached out their arms in their most ardent affection to embrace what was promised. And when one of the last of them took the child Jesus in his arms, he cried out to God, "Now dismiss your servant in peace" (Luke 2:28), as if to say, "I can die now; I've seen what my soul has always longed for."

Our present darkness and weakness in seeing the glory of Christ isn't like theirs. Their darkness came from the fact that they saw Christ in types and shadows and from an un-finished revelation. Our darkness, as we've already seen, comes from the nature of faith itself and the fact that we have to see his reflected image in the gospel, rather than face to face. But the vision of the Lamb that we'll enjoy in heaven is immeasurably clearer and greater than what we have now—so much so that the difference between the way we see Christ by faith and the way Old Testament believers saw him is almost nothing in comparison. So if they prayed and yearned to see what we see, as far greater than what they saw, how much more should we ache for our faith to become sight?

It was their wisdom to rejoice in the light they had in those ceremonies of worship that foreshadowed the glory of Christ, and to always pant after the brighter light and reve-lation of it in the gospel. In the same way it will be our wis-dom to gratefully meditate on the revelation we have of the glory of the Lamb, yet to continually pine for that perfect, that glorifying sight of him that is reserved for heaven.

At Home in the Eastern Front?

Suppose that on my sabbatical in Eastern Europe I had written to my bride something like this:

> *My dearest PJ,*
>
> *Your letters are my every delight—they overwhelm me with untold pleasures! I've grown so fond of them that I've decided to stay here in Olomouc, away from you, so that I can always enjoy them.*
>
> *Your beloved husband, etc.*

Do you think my wife would put up with such nonsense? Of course not! This isn't sweet—it's a sign of a sickness in my love for her.

If we don't love the thought of the perfect view of Christ in heaven, can we call ourselves anything but hypocrites? If we're at home in the body and would rather be away from the Lord, what can it be but a sign of a sickness in our love? What can it mean but that we cherish the world more than we do our Savior? How can anyone walk with God, or love Jesus with true faith, or find his or her greatest satisfaction and joy in spiritual things—and yet rarely meditate on the glory of Christ and long to see him face to face?

Our Lord alone perfectly understood what would make those who believe in him eternally happy, and this shaped his prayer. He cried out to God that we would be where he is and see his glory (John 17:24). If we trust him to know what's best for us, shouldn't we live in unbroken desire for what he prayed for us?

The church is often criticized these days as worldly, negligent, and powerless. If that's true, isn't it because we have deceived ourselves? We set our minds on the good life sold to us by the world, and put our faith in the bulls on Wall Street, praying that the Fed won't raise interest rates. As believers who reflect on the glory of Christ become like him (2 Corinthians 3:18), so those who set their hearts on the world become like it (Psalm 115:4–8). They become filled with vain hopes, clinging to things that will fade like the morning fog, confused and afraid, interested only in pleasing themselves.

Are you're wondering now how strong your faith is? Keep reading. . . .

For Reflection and Discussion

1. Christ is the Bridegroom of the church, his beautiful bride. As his bride, answer the question posed of the beloved in Song of Songs 5:9: "How is your beloved better than others, most beautiful of women?"

2. What does it mean that we see the glory of Christ only as a "poor reflection" (1 Corinthians 13:12) in this life?

3. What kinds of things make our view of his glory in this life clearer? Less clear?

4. What can you do in order to have a clearer view of Christ by faith?

5. Can you think of a time when you've been overwhelmed by a yearning to be with Christ face to face? Describe it.

6. What is one thing about seeing Christ face to face that you look forward to?

A long hike sometimes shows

us that we're out of shape. Maybe

all this talk of longing for Christ

has made you realize that your

heart isn't in the right place.

Let's ask ourselves some

hard questions.

[12]

My Heart Within Me
Like a Stone

*The truth is, I haven't any language weak enough to depict
the weakness of my spiritual life. If I weakened it enough it
would cease to be language at all. As when you try to turn
the gas-ring a little lower still, and it merely goes out.*
—C. S. Lewis

Aging Gracefully

Believers who are now close to leaving this world behind
have two longings. One is to recover from any spiritual decay or backsliding that has hung about them like a ball and
chain. The second is the other side of the same coin: to be
spiritually refreshed, so that they are more spiritually
minded and grow in holiness and bear fruit for the kingdom. They treasure the two sides of this coin more than the

world and everything in it. Their minds are locked on these day and night.

Refreshing grace is the only thing that can buoy us up toward the end of life, with all its troubles and temptations. Paul says that spiritual renewal kept him from losing heart as he saw his earthly life fading: "Though outwardly we are wasting away, yet inwardly we are being renewed day by day" (2 Corinthians 4:16). Troubles, especially near life's end, will overwhelm us if our hearts aren't continually renewed and revived. And hardships often increase with age. Friends die, hips break, eyes cloud over, memories come and go— until we groan with Job,

> I will die in my own house,
>> my days as numerous as the grains of sand.
>> (Job 29:18)

The only thing that can rescue us from Job's death wish is the daily spiritual renovation of the inner person.

Would it surprise you to find out that God promises to renew his gray-headed saints? The psalmist declares God's mercy in this:

> The righteous will flourish like a palm tree,
>> they will grow like a cedar of Lebanon;
> planted in the house of the LORD,
>> they will flourish in the courts of our God.
> *They will still bear fruit in old age,*
>> *they will stay fresh and green,*
> proclaiming, "The LORD is upright;

he is my Rock, and there is no wickedness in
  him."
      (Psalm 92:12–15)

This promise echoes the waterfall of promises in Psalm
72 that celebrate the days of the Messiah: "In his days the
righteous will flourish" (Psalm 72:7). It's a promise of an
overflow of grace that will pour from Christ's fullness (see
John 1:16; Colossians 1:19). This inward flourishing of
God's people is the glory of the Messiah. Where believers
are dry stumps and lifeless stones, there's no glory in the
church—no matter how beautiful their ceremonies or how
much they prosper outwardly. The glory of kings is the
wealth and peace of their subjects; the glory of Christ is the
grace and holiness of his.

The psalmist says this flourishing is like the palm tree
and its growth like the cedar. The palm tree is known for its
lush beauty and fruitfulness, and the cedar is renowned for
its towering height. So the children of the kingdom are
known for the beauty of their faith and the fruitfulness of
their obedience, as well as their constant growth and increase in grace. And this will be true for all believers, unless
by their own sinful neglect they stunt their growth and become more like scrub oak.

But the key words in Psalm 92 are in verse 14: "They will
still bear fruit *in old age,* they will stay fresh and green." This
flies in the face of nature. Aging believers will be fresh (or
"full of sap," as the NRSV has it), green, and bearing fruit.
Their freshness will come from a continual flow of the sap
of grace from Christ himself, the vine from whom they draw

the life of God (John 15:1–8). They will be green and vigorous, not withered and brittle. To their last days their limbs will be heavy with the fruit of love and obedience.

This is a promise of God. When we face natural decay and, at times, spiritual decay, he has provided in his covenant a way to make us fresh, green, and fruitful. What a privilege! It enables us even in our weakness to shout, "The LORD is upright; he is my Rock, and there is no wickedness in him" (Psalm 92:15).

Think about the burdens of old age. Imagine the frustration of forgetting things (and being aware that you're forgetting), or what it's like to wake up every day in pain, or to have to depend on someone else to bathe and dress you, or to be cut off from family and friends in a nursing home. When the faith of these believers is fresh and green and flourishing, there is no accounting for it but the faithfulness, power, and righteousness of our God.

THE PROSPERITY GOSPEL

The spiritual life that God gives us in Christ will grow and flourish until the end. That's one way to tell the difference between true faith and the "temporary faith" of hypocrites. Both may flourish and look strong at first, but temporary faith will always decay and wither (Matthew 13:20–21). Those whose spiritual life is flat (or taking a dive) should wake up now and scour their hearts to find the true nature of their faith (2 Corinthians 13:5)—because the Scriptures make it plain that spiritual life from God will grow like kudzu until the end.

We tend to slip and slide so much in our faith that we

stop expecting to grow. Or we go (spiritually) dull for so long, we think we'll never grow again the way we did when we first came to Christ. But think about what God says.

1. God compares our spiritual lives to objects that can't not grow. God calls true believers trees that are planted in good soil and well watered (Psalm 1:3). They're also like the sun that is faint at dawn but shines "ever brighter till the full light of day" (Proverbs 4:18). So the nature of true faith is to grow. If our faith is weak and dull or even stagnant, we have no evidence that we're any different from the hypocrite. The Scriptures nowhere give us any reason to rest in spiritual decay, any reason for the smug confidence that if we prayed a prayer as a child, then led a long life of indifference to God, we'll wind up in heaven. On the contrary, the Lamb of God himself threatens cold hearts:

> I know your deeds; you have a reputation of being alive, but you are dead. Wake up! Strengthen what remains and is about to die, for I have not found your deeds complete in the sight of my God. Remember, therefore, what you have received and heard; obey it, and repent. But if you do not wake up, I will come like a thief, and you will not know at what time I will come to you. (Revelation 3:1–3)

> I know your deeds, that you are neither cold nor hot. I wish you were either one or the other! So, because you are lukewarm—neither hot nor cold—I am about to spit you out of my mouth. You say, "I am

rich; I have acquired wealth and do not need a thing."
But you do not realize that you are wretched, pitiful,
poor, blind and naked. I counsel you to buy from me
gold refined in the fire, so you can become rich; and
white clothes to wear, so you can cover your shameful
nakedness; and salve to put on your eyes, so you can
see. Those whom I love I rebuke and discipline. So be
earnest, and repent. (Revelation 3:15–19)

Of course, even true believers sometimes linger under
clouds of sin and trials. But they're like the sun that is hidden behind the clouds of the storm for a while, but later
breaks out with more glory than before.

*2. God promises to give his children as much grace as
they will need to flourish right up to the end.* His promises
launch and maintain our spiritual lives. Through them we take
part in his nature (2 Peter 1:4). Consider one from Isaiah:

> For I will pour water on the thirsty land,
>   and streams on the dry ground;
> I will pour out my Spirit on your offspring,
>   and my blessing on your descendants.
> They will spring up like grass in a meadow,
>   like poplar trees by flowing streams.
>   (Isaiah 44:3–4)

If you study the context of this promise, you discover that
it is made to Israel—it's a promise of the mammoth blessings
waiting for them when they return from their exile in Baby-

lon. But the New Testament makes clear that these restoration promises are fulfilled in Christ to the Israel that is by faith. This particular promise teaches us what we are in ourselves, both before and after our conversion—we're thirsty, dry, and barren ground. In ourselves we don't have one drop of water or one sunbeam to turn us green or make our branches bend with fruit (2 Corinthians 3:5). Left to ourselves we would parch and crack like western Texas at the end of a ten-year drought. But God comes to us in Christ to pour the sanctifying water of his Spirit on us. And we'll green up like grass after the rain, and grow tall like the cottonwoods that line the banks of the Rio Grande. You can spot those cottonwoods from miles around—nothing else in the desert grows as tall. That's how we'll grow as we feed on these promises. But to feed on these promises correctly, we need to know something: God expects us to *take hold* of his promises.

There's a sense in which we aren't like trees and grass—we can't just sit and wait for God to plop these blessings on us. We're bound by God's covenant to many duties through which he fulfills these promises in us (see 2 Peter 1:4–10). This is the ordinary way we receive grace to make us flourish—our diligent obedience by faith. Sometimes God surprises us with healing grace in our backsliding (see Isaiah 57:17–18); the Good Shepherd in his sovereign mercy will go out of his way to save a wandering sheep; but the ordinary way we grow is through our obedient working out of our faith with fear and trembling.[1]

And that means that *in spite of these glorious promises, our negligence can make us spiritually weak and barren.* This is why we see such a discrepancy between the glorious gospel promises of the glory and beauty of the church, and the lives of typical Christians. We don't hold up our end, the condition of the promises.[2] We have countless promises that our spiritual lives will thrive, grow, and flourish, even in old age and up to death's door; but such grace won't fall on us while we're asleep in spiritual sloth and security.

Think of it this way: Life must be preserved by food, and God has provided the food for our spiritual lives. This food is the Word of God.

> Like newborn babies, crave pure spiritual milk, so that by it you may grow up in your salvation, now that you have tasted that the Lord is good. (1 Peter 2:2–3)

God has served up a great feast in his Word. But if we sit in front of it and refuse to eat, it's no wonder that we shrivel up like spiritual raisins. If we're too lazy to dig into his Word, or if through sin we think so little of his Word that we ignore it, how can we help but die on the vine? But God has provided all the nourishment we need, even to our last days.

THE PAINFUL REALITY

In spite of God's promises that we'll thrive, and his gracious provisions for our growth, we sometimes backslide. And those who have believed the longest are often the most susceptible—even to the kind of spiritual decay that fills us with confusion, doubt, and fear for the eternal safety of our souls.

Spiritual decay can be a slippery slope or a sheer cliff. The slippery slope is a gradual and general decline that drains all vigor from the life of grace. The sheer cliff is a sudden overwhelming temptation and fall into sin—the kind of sin that wastes the conscience and robs its peace.

Temporary believers eventually show the true colors of their hypocrisy—especially if in God's providence they face unusual prosperity or hardship. They may hang on to the outward trappings of Christianity, but their lives demonstrate nothing of God's power to make them new (Proverbs 1:31; 2 Timothy 3:5).

And temporary believers don't even know they're growing cold. Their minds are full of everything but Christ; their eyes are fixed on earthly things below, so they never see how unspiritual they are. Or, if they do sense a change, they don't care—they are spiritual sluggards who moan, "A little sleep, a little slumber, a little folding of the hands to rest" (Proverbs 6:10). But believers are restless backsliders, never really happy to be far from God. The chill in their souls pierces their hearts. Even when they fall into Satan's traps or their own flesh hoodwinks them—or when they're just plain ignorant of how to recover from spiritual decay—still their hearts can't sit still in dryness.

The Scriptures are full of believers who slide down the slippery slope or off the sheer cliff. The Lord Christ accuses five of the seven churches he addresses in Revelation 2 and 3 of slowly rotting. Some of those Christians, especially those at Sardis and Laodicea, had fallen so far that they were in danger of Christ's judgment—he threatened to remove their lampstand from its place. Haven't you seen this in your life, the casual drifting away from God until you hardly know him?

And don't you grieve over the long list of believers, many of them among the greatest followers of Christ, who inex-

plicably dove into some sin that wrecked their conscience?
My heart breaks for David as he trembles under the weight
of his sin:

> O Lᴏʀᴅ, do not rebuke me in your anger
>> or discipline me in your wrath.
> For your arrows have pierced me,
>> and your hand has come down upon me.
> Because of your wrath there is no health in my
>>> body;
>> my bones have no soundness because of my sin.
> My guilt has overwhelmed me
>> like a burden too heavy to bear.
> My wounds fester and are loathsome
>> because of my sinful folly.
>>> (Psalm 38:1–5)

When we are overcome by a grave sin or through care-
lessness continue in evil for a long time, we know God's displeasure—we can't mistake his frown. Our fear opens our
minds and hearts and shows us how sick we are. Not everyone feels it as sharply as David did in Psalm 38, because his
fall was great; but we all feel it. And each heart knows its own
bitterness (Proverbs 14:10). When we groan under such
conviction we're alone. Our hearts suffer all day long, and
others can't understand why we aren't happy. But it's better
to see believers grieving over their backsliding than to see
them falling away from God but not caring. The sad ones
are on the road to recovery; the happy-go-lucky are on the
road that leads to death.

SEARCH ME, O GOD

It's almost as hard to convince someone he's a backslider as it is for him to recover—but without the convincing, there can't be any healing. The convincing has to be the work of the Spirit (Psalm 139:23–24)—so stop now and ask for his help as you read the next few pages, and see whether he'll uncover any dryness or dullness in your heart toward Christ.

1. Ask the Spirit, "Have I slipped at all from fervent love for Christ and faithfulness to him?" I'm sure God has preserved some souls from the trap of spiritual sloth, neglect, or temptation—or at least from any long dry spells and deep valleys; but I haven't met them. There are hardly any such examples recorded in the Old Testament. In fact, almost every life recorded for us to learn from is of someone who fell (often hard) and then found help from God. Remember David's lament in Psalm 38? In Psalm 103 he celebrates his deliverance:

> Praise the LORD, O my soul,
>   and forget not all his benefits—
> who forgives all your sins
>   and heals all your diseases,
> who redeems your life from the pit
>   and crowns you with love and compassion,
> who satisfies your desires with good things
>   so that your youth is renewed like the eagle's.
>   (Psalm 103:2–5)

What kindness of God is more precious to you than his healing your spiritual sickness and restoring your spiritual strength?

Since God so often warns us of spiritual decay, and since he makes so many promises of recovery from it, and since we have so many striking examples of those who stumbled, it shouldn't surprise us that there are so many in the church every day whose hearts are dull. But what about *you?* How is it with *your* soul? Are you drifting or just going nowhere with God?

If you're confused by all this talk of backsliding—if you've never known the anguish of spiritual loss—it may be for one of two terrible reasons:

Maybe you don't feel spiritually weak because you've never been spiritually strong. Someone who has been feeble from birth doesn't know what it's like to lose his or her strength. He or she can't imagine what my friend Norman Jones must have felt. Norman as a young man was a strapping athlete, but over the years his body was slowly destroyed by multiple sclerosis.[3]

Many people take the name of Christ but don't bother to take up the life of Christ. They continue in all kinds of sins with no apparent twinges of guilt. If you try to warn them of their danger, they look at you as Lot's sons-in-law looked at him when he warned them that Sodom would be destroyed (Genesis 19:14)—as if you'd just told them the moon was made of garlic. Since they've always been the way they are, they think you're daft to talk to them about recovery—"recovery from what?" And if they've never known anything better, they'll never want to recover. If you don't think you've ever suffered spiritual decay, ask yourself honestly whether you've known spiritual strength. Or,

Maybe you don't feel spiritually weak because you're asleep at the wheel. The church of Laodicea was miles off course, yet she was so secure that she thought she was thriving in God. She thought she was rich in gifts and grace, but she was "wretched, pitiful, poor, blind and naked" (Revelation 3:17)—she was so bad off that it was hard to know whether there was any spiritual breath left in her.

God said that Ephraim (the northern kingdom of Israel) was sprinkled with gray hair, but he didn't even notice (Hosea 7:9). He was sliding downhill fast, "but despite all this he does not return to the LORD his God or search for him" (verse 10). Those who refuse to see their infection will never seek a cure (Luke 5:31–32). When a godly preacher stands in front of a congregation of such people and calls them to revival, they'll always think he's preaching about the church down the street—or they'll become indignant that he could insult them so!

2. Do you still have peace and joy? Peace and joy come from a faithful, healthy life of faith. Have your peace and joy stayed steady through hardship and temptation, or do you quickly become uneasy and confused? The peace of Christ isn't consistent with spiritual decay. If you've lost your peace, you have in some degree slipped away from Christ.

3. Do you see outward signs of decay in your spiritual life? Often we don't need to mine deep within our souls to find rot. It's lying right on the surface where anyone can see it, like the paint peeling off the walls of a house. Arrogance, selfishness, worldliness, extravagant clothing or entertainment, excessive attention to leisure,[4] vulgar or loose talk, being consumed by work or ambition—isn't it obvious that these are the ways of the world? Is this how Enoch and Abraham and Moses and David and Isaiah and Paul and John lived to please their Lord? Is this how you lived when you first came to Christ (Jeremiah 2:2)? If you understand what I'm saying, and you feel the pricking of conviction in your heart, why don't you call on the Lamb to heal you?

4. Are you tired of God? The very question should shock you—but in their sin God's people grow tired of him. Have you lost your taste for worship, either public or private? Do you neglect family prayer? Do you often find ways to justify skipping your spiritual duties?

Or, what's worse, are you still outwardly faithful in all your spiritual duties, yet as lifeless as a robot? Do you draw close to God with your lips, while your heart is in the duck blind, or on the golf course, or still in bed (Isaiah 29:13; Matthew 15:8; Mark 7:6)? I say this is worse because "God is spirit, and his worshipers must worship in spirit and in truth" (John 4:24), and because God makes such frightening threats to those whose worship is hollow (see Psalm 50). God won't be mocked.

It isn't easy to keep the mind fit for worship. It demands spiritual diligence and watchfulness, as Jesus charged his sleepy-headed disciples in the garden (Mathew 26:41). The world, the flesh, and the devil are all against you and want nothing more than to make you into a latter-day Pharisee. They use temptation to lechery, or to worldliness, or to just plain laziness to lull your spirit to sleep in a field of poppies with the Emerald City in sight. Your flesh will try to get you to rest on what you've already accomplished as a Christian (a great temptation for those who have long served God). In order to stay a step ahead of this inward persecutor, you have to strive to lay hold of God (Isaiah 64:7)—and constantly striving to lay hold of him is a sign of good spiritual health.

Another way we can lose our hearts for worship is by trying to keep a pet sin we refuse to let go of, as when Augustine prayed for God to give him sexual purity, but not just yet. Worship in spirit and truth has a great power to destroy sin. No one can worship God in spirit and truth without being broken over known sins. So in order to keep up both a secret sin and spiritual worship, worship has to be hollowed out until it's an empty shell of formalities.

5. Does the glory of God shine through you? There are graces that obviously show his glory, such as zeal for Christ, humility before God and others, brokenness over sin, a mind constantly on the things of God, love, and self-denial. Are these coursing through your veins, even if you're an older believer? Are they increasing in you (2 Peter 1:8), so that the fruit of them shows God's faithful supply of grace? Here are some ways to judge your heart in this.

How's your spiritual appetite? Do you still relish the milk of the Word of God (1 Peter 2:2–3)? I've known several people, especially those who are older, who were hospitalized because they wouldn't eat—something made them lose their taste for food. Someone who has lost his or her spiritual hunger is just as sick. Ask yourself not only whether you still want to hear the Word preached, but also whether you want it as much as you used to? And why do you want to hear preaching? Some hypocrites also want to hear preaching—so they can boast that they go to so-and-so's church, or because it entertains them, or so they can find fault with the preacher.

When people get older, they often don't want to eat as much as they used to. Food loses some of its appeal to them. The temptation might be to think that the food isn't as tasty as it used to be. But the change is in them. In the same way, if you think that the preaching isn't as good as it used to be when you were younger, ask yourself whether the change might be in your heart.

Another reason we lose our appetite is that we're stuffed. That sight of a slice of Death by Chocolate turns the stomach of someone who has gorged himself or herself on the Mexican Combination Plate. "He who is full loathes honey, but to the hungry even what is bitter tastes sweet" (Proverbs 27:7). Loss of spiritual appetite can also come from being stuffed—stuffed full of self, full of the world. But those who crave the Word find it sweet (Psalm 19:10)—so much that even its bitterest reproofs are sweet to them.

Is Christ the first and best thought of your life? When our spirits flourish, everything else in life takes a back seat to the precious Lamb of God. He sits on the throne of all we think about, long for, and do. We want to know and do what pleases him (Ephesians 5:10). But the backslider puts religion in its place. Faith is just one of many pursuits in life. It gets its one day in seven—or at least a few hours of one day in seven—and no more. God is an unwelcome intruder into business, school, friendships, entertainment.

Do you go out of your way for Christ and his people? Someone who is living in Christ bears fruit—especially the fruit of love that serves others (see John 15:1–17 in the context of John 13 and 14). When God calls you to serve, how quickly do you lift your hands? Hesitation to serve is a sign of spiritual disease.

THE TEARS OF REPENTANCE WILL WATER RENEWAL

So, did the Spirit search your heart? Did he shine his searchlight into hidden corners where it's cold or dark or dry? If so, and if your heart is softening toward Christ and longing for renewal, rejoice! This is a sign of his grace to you. Perhaps these words could serve as your prayer:

A Better Resurrection

> I have no wit, no words, no tears;
> My heart within me like a stone
> Is numb'd too much for hopes or fears;
> Look right, look left, I dwell alone;
> I lift mine eyes, but dimm'd with grief
> No everlasting hills I see;
> My life is in the falling leaf:
> O Jesus, quicken me.
>
> My life is like a faded leaf,
> My harvest dwindled to a husk:
> Truly my life is void and brief
> And tedious in the barren dusk;
> My life is like a frozen thing,
> No bud nor greenness can I see:

Yet rise it shall—the sap of Spring;
O Jesus, rise in me.

My life is like a broken bowl,
A broken bowl that cannot hold
One drop of water for my soul
Or cordial in the searching cold;
Cast in the fire the perish'd thing;
Melt and remould it, till it be
A royal cup for Him, my King:
O Jesus, drink of me.

(Christina Rossetti)

FOR REFLECTION AND DISCUSSION

1. One sign of spiritual health is that the Lamb and his Word are more precious to you than anything else. Work through Psalm 119 to see how many ways the psalmist says this. See if you can find twenty.

2. Think about a time of spiritual decay in your life. Do you remember what brought it on (either a slippery slope or a sheer cliff)? How did you know you were backsliding? What are some ways you can guard against a repeat performance?

3. Think of a time when God kept his covenant and restored you again from your backsliding. How did he rescue you? Write a six- or seven-sentence prayer of praise to him, using the details of his rescue operation.

Finally, to all who
have slipped from the path,
God reaches down his
strong hand to help.

[1 3]

Parched and Ravenous
I Seek Him

When I deserved it least, God gave me most.
I think it was the Savior's face itself I saw.
—Frederick Buechner

BABETTE'S FEAST

Isak Dinesen's delicious short story tells of a puritanical sect in Norway that was started by a prophet they called the Dean. The little community of believers thrived during the Dean's lifetime, but in the years after his death the group dwindled, and those who remain have become "somewhat querulous and quarrelsome, so that sad little schisms would arise in the congregation." Martine and Philippa, the Dean's two daughters, do their best to keep the brothers and sisters together, but this is clearly a church in spiritual decay.

But then Babette wins the French lottery.

Babette is the maid and cook who has humbly served Martine and Philippa for years and conceals a secret past: no one knows that she was once a great chef at the *Café Anglais* in Paris, who could turn a dinner into "a kind of love affair." Because Babette no longer has a family in Paris to return to, she decides to spend every franc of her winnings on one meal for the remaining disciples and the aging General Loewenhielm, who has come to the point in his life where he wonders about his eternal destiny.

Babette recreates for these simple folk one of her renowned masterpieces, *Cailles en Sarcophage*. She orders a sea turtle and makes turtle soup. She serves the finest Amontillado the general has ever tasted (and he is one who is suspicious of his wine), and follows it with a Veuve Cliquot 1860. She lays before them quails and pastries and fresh fruits. It is glorious.

Something happens during the meal.

> The eldest member of the congregation said grace in the Dean's own words. . . . An old brother told the story of his first meeting with the Dean. Another went through that sermon which sixty years ago had brought about his conversion. . . . A sister on the other side of the table opened the subject of strange happenings which had taken place while the Dean was still amongst his children, and which one might venture to call miracles.[1]

As they reflect on the life and teachings of the Dean and feast on Babette's grace, "Taciturn old people received the gift of tongues; ears that for years had been almost deaf were opened to it. Time itself had merged into eternity. Long after midnight the windows of the house shone like gold, and golden song flowed out into the winter air." Long-broken friendships are mended with warm hugs, and bursts of laughter take the place of deep-rooted grudges. As the narrator put it, "They had been given one hour of the millennium."

Even in their dying years, these old believers are restored.

What's told here so well in fiction, delightfully portrays what God declares for his backsliding people.

THERE'S HOPE AHEAD

God intends for us not just to survive, not just to hang on by our fingernails until the end, but to thrive in him. He's provided everything we need to recover from spiritual decay and grow in Christ, even to the very end of our days on earth. You can't say there's no hope in Christ—that denies the gospel and calls God a liar. In the previous chapter we looked at just a few of his promises to revive us—but there are plenty more where those came from. If every backward step we took on the way to heaven were unrecoverable, we'd all go up in smoke! If God marked all our slips and stumbles, "O Lord, who could stand?" (Psalm 130:3). If we didn't have help from our failures *every day*, we'd be in a spiritual free fall without a parachute.

So our first job is to hope—and to hope with a hope that won't disappoint us (Romans 5:5).

THERE'S HARD WORK AHEAD

Spiritual recovery is hard work. Yes, all the praise for any health or growth or strength is due to God alone: "Not to us, O LORD, not to us but to your name be the glory, because of your love and faithfulness" (Psalm 115:1). But as we said in chapter 12, God works through ordinary means, and the ordinary way we recover is through the demanding work of killing the flesh.

> For if you live according to the [flesh], you will die; but if by the Spirit you put to death the misdeeds of the body, you will live. . . . (Romans 8:13)

It's beyond my scope in this book to cover the details of how to defeat the flesh,[2] but I'll offer two warnings.

First, make sure that you attack the flesh with God's weapons and not your own. You'll find lots of teachers in churches who offer remedies that don't come from God. When we try to offer them to God he says to us, "Who has asked this of you?" (Isaiah 1:12). The Pharisees, for example, were notorious for piling high the works and duties that would win God's pleasure, yet few of those works came from God. And the church has added its share of fastings, pilgrimages, abstinence, prayers, and rituals that have little or no basis in God's Word. Paul's condemnation of them is enough:

> These are all destined to perish with use, because they are based on human commands and teachings.

Such regulations indeed have an appearance of wisdom, with their self-imposed worship, their false humility and their harsh treatment of the body, but they lack any value in restraining sensual indulgence. (Colossians 2:22–23)

The problem is that we naturally run to these man-made solutions. When we're convinced we're backsliders, we feel the guilt of sin and want relief for our consciences. So we look for a way to atone God's anger and be accepted by him—and if we aren't guided by the gospel in this, our flesh will offer two kinds of suggestions. The first is some extraordinary duty or service that God never asked of us, such as fasting for a week or not eating ice cream for a year. The second is an extraordinary multiplication of duties beyond what God commands. There's an example of both of these in Micah:

> With what shall I come before the LORD
>   and bow down before the exalted God?
> Shall I come before him with burnt offerings,
>   with calves a year old?
> Will the LORD be pleased with *thousands of rams,*
>   with *ten thousand rivers of oil?*
> *Shall I offer my firstborn for my transgression,*
>   *the fruit of my body for the sin of my soul?*
>   (Micah 6:6–7)

Sometimes our guilt hurts so much that we madly want to do something extraordinary to make the pain stop. But what does God require of us for our spiritual recovery? Simple: renewed obedience in *his* means of killing the flesh. His means are those outlined throughout his Word and they're familiar: constantly reading his Word, hearing it preached, and reflecting on it;[3] fervent prayer; careful watching against temptation; and fixing the mind always on things above, where Christ is seated at the right hand of God.

Second, always attack the flesh by the power of the Spirit (Romans 8:13), in dependence on Christ (1 Corinthians 15:10). The Spirit rejects self-confidence and independence, and we'll never prosper by trying to obey God's commands in our own strength (2 Corinthians 3:5; 9:8)—that's not gospel obedience. Too many people pray and read and fast and give to the poor and struggle to resist temptation by mere self-control—like the man in the commercial who clenches his fists and screws up his face in determination and says, "I will not cough, I will not cough." Cough.

This leaves Christ out of the picture, and leaves us floundering. But listen to your Lord:

> If you listen carefully to the voice of the LORD your God and do what is right in his eyes, if you pay attention to his commands and keep all his decrees, I will not bring on you any of the diseases I brought on the Egyptians, for *I am the LORD, who heals you.* (Exodus 15:26)

And when we attack the flesh in our own strength, the worst thing that can happen is anything that might smell like success—because our pride will jump to make a merit badge out of it. We'll begin to justify ourselves before God, and that will lead us away from sincere faith, away from the gospel, away from Christ. But faith clings to Christ in everything and won't move an inch without his help. Faith won't read a chapter, sing a hymn, say a prayer, or offer a gift, without calling on the strength of Christ by the Spirit. This is what it means to live by faith in the Son of God (Galatians 2:20). And when we live this way, God always revives us.

I Am the Lord, Who Heals You

Because we so easily backslide and decay, God has given us great and precious promises of a recovery—if we duly apply ourselves to his means. In chapter 12 we glanced at a few of these promises. Now let's linger over one for a while and see what we can learn about spiritual healing:

> Return, O Israel, to the LORD your God.
>> Your sins have been your downfall!
> Take words with you
>> and return to the LORD.
> Say to him:
>> "Forgive all our sins
> and receive us graciously,
>> that we may offer the fruit of our lips.
> Assyria cannot save us;
>> we will not mount war-horses.
> We will never again say 'Our gods'
>> to what our own hands have made,
>> for in you the fatherless find compassion."

"I will heal their waywardness
   and love them freely,
     for my anger has turned away from them.
I will be like the dew to Israel;
   he will blossom like a lily.
Like a cedar of Lebanon
   he will send down his roots;
     his young shoots will grow.
His splendor will be like an olive tree,
   his fragrance like a cedar of Lebanon.
Men will dwell again in his shade.
   He will flourish like the grain.
He will blossom like a vine,
   and his fame will be like the wine from Lebanon.
O Ephraim, what more have I to do with idols?
   I will answer him and care for him.
I am like a green pine tree;
   your fruitfulness comes from me."
                    (Hosea 14:1–8)

God doesn't abandon his wandering children, but calls them to *return*. In the last words before those above (the end of Hosea 13), we learn that most of the people were under God's threat because of their wickedness—and it wasn't long after this that God made good his threat. Isn't this striking? Even in the middle of the extreme wickedness of his people, even in the same breath that he threatens to dash their babies to the ground and rip open their pregnant women (Hosea 13:16), he offers his mercy. Remember that Jesus deals the same with the wretched church at Laodicea in Revelation 3:14–21. No one who belongs to God is beyond the reach of his grace.

In times of widespread apostasy like this, even true believers can be swept along with the sins of the masses and suffer spiritual decay: "Because of the increase of wickedness, the love of most will grow cold" (Matthew 24:12). This happened to the true Israelites, although they hadn't completely broken their covenant with God. He still called himself "the LORD your God," even though their sin was great.

When God plans to revive us, he calls us to use his means for our healing: "Take words with you and return to the LORD" (Hosea 14:2). In other words, God calls us to renew our repentance. Specifically, he calls us to *fervent* prayer. Don't take your danger too lightly. Remember that you're dealing with God, and that "it is a dreadful thing to fall into the hands of the living God" (Hebrews 10:31). And take care to make a full confession, and look for God's pardon from *all* your sins (Hosea 14:2). Don't hang onto even one pet sin and try to smuggle it into God's presence. He won't be fooled. Take every sin to him and ask for nothing but grace: "Receive us graciously" (Hosea 14:2). Ask God to show his mercy, to let you know in your heart that he has accepted you.

In order to take all your sins to God, make your confession *specific*. Hosea said Israel should confess her dependence on man and her idolatry (14:3). These were the popular sins of the day, and even true Israelites had been caught up in them. God expected a full confession.

More than a renewal of repentance, God expects us to renew our faith in him. In Hosea 14:3 he told Israel to confess God's mercy as the foundation of their hope: "In you the fatherless find compassion." And out of renewed repentance and faith should flow our praise and thanksgiving, which is the purpose of God's healing us: "that we may offer the fruit of our lips" (Hosea 14:2).[4] In fact, when God repairs our spiritual decay and heals our backsliding through these means, he does it in such a way that he may pour his grace on us to the praise of his own glory. That's why he prescribes these duties to us. Our obedience isn't the *cause* of his love and grace that heals us, yet he requires it; through it he dispenses grace. Here, as always in the Bible, there's a mysterious harmony between God's sovereign grace ("I will heal their waywardness and love them freely," verse 3) and our diligent duty ("Return," "take words," verse 1).[5]

Since this is the way God deals with us, we can't expect to recover unless we find these things worked in our hearts: sincere prayer, thorough confession and repentance, fresh faith and praise to God. We have no reason to hope that if we continue to be spiritual sluggards and pigs, wallowing in the mud of worldliness, God will pop in uninvited and fix us up. If he worked that way, without showing us our danger and convicting us of our sin, how would we ever know to thank him?

And how we should thank him! Backsliding isn't a hangnail—it's a cancer that weakens our souls and will certainly destroy us if God doesn't heal us. Because the sin of backsliding is so dangerous to our souls, the Bible often calls recovery from it "healing" (see Psalm 6:2; Isaiah 57:18–19; Hosea 6:1). In Hosea 14 the healing (verse 4) includes pardon of past sin and a new supply of grace for fruitful obedience (verses 4–7). This healing flows only from God's grace (verse 4), and it flows like the mighty river of metaphors in verses 5–7 that paint such a lavish picture of God's healing.

This glorious healing is what we can hope for and expect from our God.

SPIRITUAL RENEWAL AND THE GLORY OF CHRIST

Since we spent chapter 12 asking the Spirit to search us and tell us whether we're backsliders, you may think we've lost our focus on the glory of Christ. But when we answer the question, "How do I recover from spiritual decay?" we find ourselves right back where we started this book. You see, there can't be any real revival apart from the glory of Christ.

Every ounce of grace we receive comes from Jesus Christ. As we've seen in Hosea 14, the Old Testament promises grace; but the way we receive it is revealed in the New. Jesus assures us that without him we can't lift a finger. Like a branch hacked away from the vine, apart from him we can't produce even the most shriveled piece of fruit (John 15:3–5). He's our head, and we're the body. Separate the two and what do you have? He is our life, and he powers every useful spiritual move we make (Galatians 2:20; Colossians 3:1–4).

Are you at all stirred by a conviction that your spiritual life is languishing? Do you yearn for a renewal of spiritual strength that will flourish in faith, love, and holiness? Then drive a stake into this solid ground: you won't have a bit of it apart from Jesus. You can claim every promise in the Book and screw up your courage to carry out the toughest spiritual disciplines—but you won't find a breath of relief unless

Christ breathes on you. And if we can only be renewed through Christ, isn't he glorious?

Every ounce of grace we receive comes by faith. By faith we come to Christ, are planted in Christ, and live in Christ to bear fruit for him. By our faith he lives in us and acts in us, so that we live by faith in the Son of God. You won't find a jot or tittle in the Scriptures to suggest that you'll receive anything from Christ other than by faith. Faith points away from us and our strength to Christ and his glory.

This faith is in the person of Christ, his grace, all his work to bring us to God, and his glory in everything. We end this book where we began: What we need more than all the wisdom and wealth of the world is a steady view by faith of the glory of the Lamb as he's revealed to us in his Word. It's the only medicine to heal our sick souls, and the only true fountain of youth to keep our spirits fresh even in old age.

> Those who look to him are radiant;
>> their faces are never covered with shame.
>> (Psalm 34:5)

What's a better expression of faith in Christ than to believe that looking at him will refresh us? Or what better work of faith than looking at his glory? Isn't this the ultimate confidence in him?

Spiritual recovery begins and continues when we gaze on the glory of Christ (2 Corinthians 3:18). It changes us every day more and more into his image through the looking glass of the Scriptures, as we've already seen. If you've ever been revived, it was through a clearer and more constant view of Christ. If you're ever going to be renewed again, it will happen when you see his glory. Haven't we tried enough religious gimmicks to prop up our faith? Isn't it time we turn our eyes once again to the one who saved us, and let his beauty overwhelm us? What would the church be like if all of us kept the eyes of our faith ever fixed on the glory of the Lamb?

May it be so with you.

May it be so with me.

As a Stranger

As a stranger here I wander in a wasteland, vast and
     void,
worn and weary, pressing onward, gazing at my
     Lord.
Parched and ravenous I seek him, waiting, kneeling
     at his throne;
panting as a hart for water, my heart pants for God
     alone.

May I dwell among the faithful who delight them-
     selves in Christ,
longing only for his presence, seeking paradise.
Turn our eyes away from idols; fix our vision on
     you, Lord;
may we only seek the treasure of your holy, living
     Word.

Burning, yearning for my Jesus, groaning in this
mortal jail;
my soul is consumed with longing till death re-
moves the veil.
When we're clothed with him in heaven we will see
him face to face;
we will ever dwell before him, brought there by his
sovereign grace.

For Reflection and Discussion

1. One of the points we drew from Hosea 14 is that when
   his people are wallowing in unthinkable sin, God
   reaches out to them in their darkness and calls them
   back to himself. Think about some of the sins that people like Noah and Moses and Abraham and Samson
   and David and Peter fell into—yet God held out his
   hands to them. How does this show his glory?

2. Describe in your own words how our hard work and
   God's sovereign mercy work together to bring our renewal.

3. How is it that our spiritual renewal brings glory and
   honor to Christ?

4. This is the final exam for the whole book: How is it that
   seeing the glory of Christ brings our spiritual renewal?

Notes

Chapter 1: To See His Glory

1 I was practicing the shot put.

2 See Isaiah 33:17.

3 We'll still be creatures in heaven, and so we'll still have limits. But we'll be far less limited than we are now. For example, we won't be limited by sin or our flesh.

4 Augustine, *Confessions* 1.1.

5 The NIV says in this verse that we reflect the glory of the Lord, rather than reflect on it. Although I'm no Greek scholar, I suspect it is wrong. See the NIV footnote on this verse, and look at every other translation.

6 Matthew 8:20.

7 John Owen, *The Glory of Christ*, in volume 6 of his *Works*, ed. William Goold (Edinburgh: Johnstone and Hunter, 1850–53).

8 See Colossians 3:1–17, especially verses 1 and 15; also Hebrews 12:2–3.

9 If you know nothing of this peace, you must seriously ask yourself whether you are blind to Christ. If you are, come to him by faith—and he'll give you himself even now!

10 We could call this "sanctification by contemplation."

Chapter 2: The Only Face of God

1   C. S. Lewis, *The Last Battle* (New York: Macmillan, 1956), 155–57.

2   See Exodus 20:21; Deuteronomy 5:22; 1 Kings 8:12; 2 Chronicles 6:1.

3   See John 1:5,14,17–18; 2 Corinthians 4:3–4.

4   For a detailed discussion of how Christ was prefigured in Old Testament worship and law, see Vern S. Poythress, *The Shadow of Christ in the Law of Moses* (Brentwood, Tenn.: Wolgemuth & Hyatt, 1991; Phillipsburg, N.J.: P&R Publishing, 1995).

5   C. S. Lewis, *Mere Christianity* (New York: MacMillan, 1952), 135.

6   For some helpful instruction in this, see Richard L. Pratt, Jr., *Pray with Your Eyes Open* (Phillipsburg, N.J.: Presbyterian and Reformed, 1987), chapter 4.

Chapter 3: Lost in a Mystery

1   *O altitudo* is the Latin phrase that begins the Vulgate version of Romans 11:33: "Oh, the depth of the riches of the wisdom and knowledge of God!" It expresses how Paul was swept away by wonder as he swam in the depths of God's wisdom.

2   See also Psalms 29:3, 10; 65:7.

3   With this offering I'm trying to reconcile myself to fans of Lewis.

4   Lewis, *The Lion, The Witch, and The Wardrobe* (New York: Macmillan, 1950), 133. The emphasis is mine.

5   Many books of theology can help you if you aren't acquainted with the Christian doctrine of the person of

Christ. I list a few at the end of this chapter, in the "For Reflection and Discussion" section. And you'll be well rewarded if you have the patience and strength to work through John Owen's *ΧΡΙΣΤΟΛΟΓΙΑ: or, a Declaration of the Glorious Mystery of the Person of Christ,* in volume 1 of his *Works,* ed. William Goold (Edinburgh: Johnstone and Hunter, 1850–53).

6   Compare Philippians 4:8.

7   See, among other places, Genesis 3:15; Psalms 2:7–9; 45:2–6; 68:17–18; 110; Isaiah 6:1–4; 9:6; Zechariah 3:8; John 1:1–3; Philippians 2:6–8; Hebrews 1:1–3; 2:14–16; Revelation 1:17–18.

8   See, for example, Genesis 49:10; 1 Samuel 2:10; Job 19:25; Psalms 40:6–10 (compare what is said about these verses in Hebrews 10:5–10); 118:22–26; Isaiah 11:1–10; 40:11; 42:1–4; 49:1–12; 55:3–5; 59:16–20; Jeremiah 23:5–6; 33:15–18; Daniel 7:13–14; Haggai 2:7; Malachi 4:2.

9   For help with this see my *The Enemy Within: Straight Talk About the Power and Defeat of Sin* (Phillipsburg, N.J.: P&R Publishing, 1998). Or go straight to Owen's writings on sin in volume 6 of his *Works.*

10 See also Song of Songs 5:2–8.

Chapter 4: He Stoops Down to Look on the Heavens

1   This isn't a reason to stop saying creeds. It's a reason to repent of our hard hearts.

2   My tongue is in my cheek.

3   See Genesis 3:24.

4   See 1 Samuel 2:25.

5   I have a daughter too, but she isn't part of this story.

6   I can only mention these in passing and trust you to explore them in more detail as you get to know Christ more clearly. I recommend Jack Rogers et al., *Case Studies in Christ and Salvation* (Philadelphia: Westminster Press, 1977), 19–42, and Harold O. J. Brown, *Heresies: The Image of Christ in the Mirror of Heresy and Orthodoxy from the Apostles to the Present* (Grand Rapids: Baker, 1984), 95–195.

7   It's beyond my scope (and my skill) to fully exegete Philippians 2:6–8. I refer you to the best commentary that I've seen on this: Moisés Silva, *The Wycliffe Exegetical Commentary: Philippians* (Chicago: Moody Press, 1988), 112–26.

8   Compare Philippians 2:6 in the NRSV, and in the context of Paul's purpose in 2:5. He is teaching us not to be self-serving, and showing us how Christ refused to act selfishly. In his humility Christ didn't use his equality with God for his own advantage.

Chapter 5: The River of Love

1   From an anonymous fourteenth-century poem translated by Donald Davie in Donald Davie, ed., *The New Oxford Book of Christian Verse* (Oxford: Oxford University Press, 1981), 7.

2   "Body" here represents his entire human nature, body and spirit.

Chapter 6: A Hero to Worship

1   I speak, of course, of the Doc Savage of Kenneth Robeson in the 1920s and 1930s—not the fallen modern incarnation of Doc Savage by Philip Jose Farmer!

2   Matthew 26:36–46; Mark 14:32–42; Luke 22:39–48.

3   I've followed the modernized spelling and capitalization
    used by Louis L. Martz in *The Oxford Poetry Library: George
    Herbert* (Oxford: Oxford University Press, 1994), 18.

Chapter 7: God's Right-Hand Man
1   From *Henry V*, 4.0.
2   Ibid., 4.1.

Chapter 8: The Center of the Old Testament
1   Vern S. Poythress, *The Shadow of Christ in the Law of Moses*
    (Brentwood, Tenn.: Wolgemuth & Hyatt, 1991; Phillips-
    burg, N.J.: P&R Publishing, 1995), 38.
2   Ibid.
3   See, for example, John 1:29, 36; 6:32–35; 1 Corinthians
    5:7; Colossians 2:17; Hebrews 4:14–16; 5:1–10; 8:2;
    9:7–15, 18–28; 10:19–22; 13:10–13; 1 Peter 1:18–19. Ob-
    viously, a solid commentary on Hebrews would be a use-
    ful secondary source.
4   See also, for example, Isaiah 49:8; 61:10; Jeremiah 2:2;
    Ezekiel 16:8–14.
5   And, I assume, twenty-first-century.
6   You need look no further than Jonathan Edwards and
    our beloved John Owen himself to find examples.
7   From *Divine Hymns or Spiritual Songs,* comp. Joshua
    Smith (New Hampshire, 1784).
8   See Charles Hodge, *Systematic Theology,* 3 vols. (Reprint.
    Grand Rapids: Eerdmans, 1982), 1:484–95.

Chapter 9: By Just Exchange
1   Victor Hugo, *Les Miserables*, 1.7.3.

2   This is why the priest was to lay his hand on the head of the sacrifice, symbolizing the transfer of the guilt of the people to the animal. See Leviticus 3–4.

3   See, in particular, chapter 6.

4   Every sin ever committed is punished—either in Christ as he hangs on the cross for his people or by the sinner in hell forever.

5   John Owen, *The Glory of Christ*, in volume 6 of his *Works*, ed. William Goold (Edinburgh: Johnstone and Hunter, 1850–53), 359.

6   This is the doctrine of "original sin," or the corruption of our nature. For an extensive exposition of this doctrine, see Jonathan Edwards, *The Great Christian Doctrine of Original Sin Defended; Evidences of Its Truth Produced, and Arguments to the Contrary Answered* (1758). For a summary, see Louis Berkhof, *Systematic Theology* (Grand Rapids: Eerdmans, 1941), 244–54.

Chapter 10: The Glory of Glories

1   I suppose some scientist is in a lab somewhere working on it with grant money.

2   "Everything's Broken," *Oh Mercy*, © 1989 CBS Records Inc.

3   See chapter 2.

Chapter 12: My Heart Within Me Like a Stone

1   See the Westminster Confession of Faith, 5.3: "God, in His ordinary providence, makes use of means, yet is free to work without, above, and against them, at His pleasure."

2   I'm not suggesting that our obedience merits God's favor. Our ability to obey comes from him, so how can it

merit anything more from him? This is a matter of covenant, what he requires of us.

3   I've never met anyone who was a better example of someone who was outwardly wasting away, but inwardly renewed every day. Norman taught me a lot about God's grace.

4   Leisure can of course be spent doing good to others or strengthening yourself for service to God. But here I mean it in the sense of pastimes that are mere diversions—like watching *Who Wants to Be a Millionaire?*

Chapter 13: Parched and Ravenous I Seek Him

1   Isak Dinesen, "Babette's Feast," first published in 1958 in *Anecdotes of Destiny*. Republished in *Anecdotes of Destiny and Ehrengard* (New York: Vintage Books, 1993).

2   There is no better help for this in all of Christian literature than John Owen's *Mortification of Sin*, in volume 6 of his *Works*. If you don't have the patience to work through his ponderous prose, you're welcome to try my *The Enemy Within: Straight Talk About the Power and Defeat of Sin* (Phillipsburg, N.J.: P&R Publishing, 1998). It's not as thorough, but covers his best points in simpler language.

3   Reading the Bible and sitting in front of a preacher aren't the same as meditating on God's Word. Read Psalm 119 and ask yourself how many times this lover of the Word rejoices to *read* it. (You won't find any.)

4   "Will you not revive us again, that your people may rejoice in you?" (Psalm 85:6).

5   Compare Philippians 2:12–13.